"Politano's communication style is clear, precise and practical. There's no one better at staying ahead of the Business Intelligence curve in a pragmatic way. He's a Business Intelligence leader."

—Sam Friedlander
Manager, Business Intelligence/Data Warehousing
Sybase

Chief Performance Officer is a clear and comprehensive account of an organization and process that companies have needed for years. Politano's consulting experience gives his research immense credibility. Anyone interested in leveraging information across his or her firm will gain a great deal from this book."

—Jerry Luftman
Executive Director
Graduate IS Programs
Stevens Institute of Technology

"Tony lucidly lays out a compelling roadmap of how any company can understand, measure, and drive business performance, regardless of where they are in their performance or information technology evolution. In addition, he provides the tools that enable business performance measurement and analysis."

—Jeff Reaves
Finance Director
Ticona

"That the Chief Performance Officer doesn't yet exist hasn't stopped Tony Politano from meditating on this "executive's" responsibilities. The trick, and one I think Politano has successfully pulled off, is to place the burden of measuring, monitoring, and managing the performance of the entire enterprise on the shoulders of one person, then figure out how to use old-fashioned hard work, business ingenuity, and technology to lift that burden. What remains to be seen is just how fast—and to what depth—corporations accept the accurate assessment and vision embodied in Mr. Politano's work."

—Robert Moran
Vice President/Managing Director, Data Knowledge &
Aberdeen Group

CHIEF PERFORMANCE OFFICER

CHIEF PERFORMANCE OFFICER

Measuring What Matters, Managing
What Can Be Measured

Anthony L. Politano

iUniverse, Inc.
New York Lincoln Shanghai

CHIEF PERFORMANCE OFFICER
Measuring What Matters, Managing What Can Be Measured

iUniverse, Inc.

For information address:
iUniverse, Inc.
2021 Pine Lake Road, Suite 100
Lincoln, NE 68512
www.iuniverse.com

ISBN: 0-595-28057-9

Printed in the United States of America

To my wife Bonnie. We both speak the international language. You know—love.

In memory of Bob Moran of Aberdeen Group. Visionary, mentor and friend

Contents

Acknowledgements

I would like to thank, first and foremost, my wife, Bonnie, for her support throughout this and so many of my other projects. Besides being the love of my life, her background, and our shared time at James Martin & Co, makes her the perfect reality check when my ideas go too far "out there."

It also gives me pleasure to thank all the people who are part of my academic life, including Professors Sack and Luftman, the faculty and staff at Stevens Institute in Hoboken, and "Doc" Bob Bunio from Columbia High School, who got me started on this computer centric career trek in 1979.

Thank you to my business partner, Herbert Birman, colleagues, and co-workers, worldwide at MIS AG. It is great to work with a group of people who "get it." Thanks, Doug Conway for my first real job, way back in controllers systems at Pru. Who knew it would end up here?

To all the people who have contributed to, reviewed, or edited this book, thank you. A special thanks to Arlene Uhl and Jeanne Achille from The Devon Group.

Thank you to my uncle, the Honorable Nicholas H. Politan, and to my Army Drill Sergeant Pierce for demonstrating what true service to your country means. And thanks to Fathers Ron and John from the Newman Center, who still inspire me.

Finally, thank you to my Mom, Dad, grandparents, and the United States for giving me the opportunity to have such a wonderful and rewarding career.

Foreword

Organizations continue to experience profound change. In the last two years alone, the United States has encountered recession, terrorism, downsizing, Enronitis, war, government deficits, and SARS. The Information Technology (IT) function has been greatly impacted by all of them. Additionally, over the years, IT has experienced major shifts in the technology they support and the services they provide. Companies are starting to recognize the value that IT can provide in the attainment of business strategies in this ever increasingly dynamic environment.

One area, data and data warehousing, has remained an elusive strategy for almost four decades. It is true that the technology continues to evolve, but not quite in the areas that are most crucial. Research in assessing IT-business Alignment Maturity has demonstrated that there are six areas that all must be worked on concurrently to ensure the appropriate relationship across IT and business organizations. The components are:

1. Communications

2. Value Metrics

3. IT Governance

4. Partnership

5. Technology

6. Human Resources

Technology is only one of six areas that need to be addressed. In the past, organizations have put too much emphasis on the "correct" technology, and not enough emphasis on all of the remaining five. This book presents effective organizational and procedural systems that seek to ensure all aspects of success in leveraging the most valuable corporate asset—data.

Politano starts by defining the important new roles, skills, and measurements for the Chief Performance Officer (CPO). He then describes the processes and techniques necessary to achieve critical goals. Most important is the need to understand the degree of data sharing and data availability that exists and needs to exist within the firm and across external customers and partners. To accomplish this demands a mature IT-business relationship. IT cannot do this alone. Too often IT is given the responsibility of implementing an ERP that will provide an integrated Customer Relationship Management and/or Supply Chain Management system. If technology is not implemented with organizational and procedural changes in mind, the project will have little chance for success. Politano discusses important approaches to addressing some of these pervasive problems.

He goes further by describing activities to leverage the data that exists. Opportunities such as business intelligence, key performance indicators (KPI), benchmarking, scenario planning, data mining, and delta mining, to name a few, can provide important insights when making real-time business decisions. Too often, firms do not take advantage of their data assets. This requires a strong IT-business facilitator, the Chief Performance Officer.

Jerry Luftman
Executive Director
Graduate IS Programs
Stevens Institute of Technology

Introduction: Why Have a Chief Performance Officer?

Public or private. Regional or Global. Manufacturing or Services. Brick and Mortar or Click and Mortar. Growing or Stabilized. For Profit or Not for Profit. In my twenty years of dealing with corporations, there is one unequivocal fact: increase corporate performance and you will increase stakeholder value.

The industry's solution to increasing performance, though, has been fragmented, at best. The chief financial officer utilizes tighter controls or new techniques, such as activity-based costing. The chief information officer introduces Enterprise Resource Planning systems and Data Warehouses. Executive sales management performs frequent reorganizations and alignments. The supply chain executive implements just-in-time inventory systems and consolidates warehouses.

It is rare that an organization takes the holistic view that managing performance touches all parts of the organization. There needs to be a chief to manage performance, thus the role of the chief performance officer (CPO).

Some organizations are performing the role of the chief performance officer through a group or committee. Others see this as another job of the CFO or CIO. However, there are two key factors: accountability and empowerment.

The CPO must be accountable for measuring all areas of corporate performance. He or she must also be empowered by the CEO to pull this information from the various business silos that exist in a typical organization.

As an emerging role, the CPO requires a method to perform day-to-day duties, as well as strategic ones. In this book, we fully define the role of the CPO: the required skills sets, the methods the CPO uses, the breadth and depth of the CPO's responsibility, the interaction points with the various business areas, and ways to measure the success of the CPO.

Various real-life examples are included in each chapter to highlight specific examples of how leading organizations are implementing the CPO, in whole or in part. Upon completion of this book, the reader should have a clear understanding of how a CPO in any size organization will lead to tangible increases in corporate performance and increased stakeholder value.

1

The Chief Performance Officer—A Heads-Up Display for the CEO

Fighter pilots traveling at supersonic speeds rely heavily on their displays and gauges. Split-second decisions need to be made in real time. Their data-monitoring needs are intensive: from weapons systems to power plant to radar images to navigation systems. Basing decisions on the wrong data can prove fatal.

Chief Executives also require data and input from their organization. They need to make critical decisions based on this data. Basing decisions on incomplete or faulty data can prove to be devastating for the organization and the CEO's career.

Just as the fighter pilot relies on a heads-up display, the CEO's needs are similar. But, since the data the CEO needs to make decisions is disparate in both a business context and with regard to technical systems, it is not as simple as adding a heads-up display. Technology currently exists to provide CEO-level dashboards, but the real heads-up display is an emerging role in organizations, the chief performance officer (CPO).

The CPO acts as the heads-up display for the CEO. And similar to the fighter pilot, actions are taken based on indications from that display. Since much of the data required for decisions is business specific, the CPO must be specialized enough to provide a relevant context to the required data.

In many organizations, multiple individuals are actually playing the CPO role. Chief financial officers (CFO) provide the much needed input from a financial perspective such as revenue, margin, EBIT, etc. Supply chain executives provide needed input from vendors and give perspective, including lead times, turn around, etc. Research & development, customer support and human resources have their own measurements, as well.

In reality, though, the CEO ends up being the integrator and interpreter of the information. The CEO must take in information from various reports, graphs, and presentations and correlate this information to make informed decisions. There are two major problems with this scenario. First, the CEO may not have intimate enough knowledge of the data to perform adequate correlation of disjoint business data. Second, and more important, the CEO does not have the time for these tasks. In the fighter jet, the jet pilot does not use wind gauges, compasses, dipsticks, and voltmeters to gather the information while flying at Mach 2. The pilot is presented with the most relevant data required to make the decision at that exact moment. CEOs need this type of heads-up functionality for their business.

THE CPO: BUSINESS EXECUTIVE, TECHNOLOGIST, INTERPRETER

The CPO is faced with the unique challenge of being part business executive, part technologist, and part interpreter.

First, business expertise and business experience are paramount for the CPO. A thorough and complete understanding of the strategy of the business is required. The CPO must have expertise that can help him to understand not just what is happening in the organization, but why. Through this expertise, the CPO can identify and make relevant disjointed observations from the business data. The CPO also needs real business experience. This is not a role for fresh-out-of-college hires.

There are certain intangible business skills that are only gained through experience.

As part of the expertise, the CPO must have analytical tools such as forecasting, strategic planning, return-on-investment models, and governance compliance. These raw tools are most likely being used by various parts of the organization, and the CPO will need a certain understanding of all of them.

Second, the CPO is part technologist. A successful CPO has technical knowledge, but is not burdened with technical implementation details. Unlike a chief technology officer (CTO) or chief information officer (CIO) who may implement programs for 'technical glory,' the CPO is interested in technical pragmatism. The CPO must be aware of the existing technology used by management such as budgeting systems, data warehouses, and intranets. Detailed technical knowledge of the inner workings in not necessary, though, since the CPO is ultimately interested in the output, or data, drawn from these systems. The CPO must also understand emerging trends in technology. Of particular interest are areas such as business intelligence, which concentrates on collecting and disseminating analytical business data, and collaborative systems, which allow automated sharing of information throughout the organization through Web-based technologies.

It is also important for the CPO to understand the importance of introducing technology incrementally. Too many information technology project sponsors underestimate the impact of 'technical saturation.' To a pure technologist, the latest Java-based, Web-enabled, thin-client application may be the best answer, but to the actual business user of the system, an extension to their existing spreadsheet might accomplish the same end. The CPO ultimately represents the business, and cannot be lured into the trap of looking for 'technical glory.'

Third, the CPO is part interpreter. The CPO must be able to communicate in both business and technical terms. Concurrently, he or she must be able to speak at different levels of detail, whether at a management, executive, or board level. The CPO must have the vocabulary and interpretive knowledge to bring the information to the recipient's level. It does little or no good to present middle-management level project statistics at a board of directors meeting. Conversely, middle management may not understand or be privy to board-level aggregated performance data. As interpreter, the CPO must quickly be able to adjust the level and context of what is being presented.

THE 4 C'S: THE ROLES OF THE CPO

The roles of the CPO can be classified into four categories: collector, consolidator, condenser, and communicator. In performing each of these roles, the CPO can provide significant value to an organization.

Collector

The CPO plays the role of collector. He or she collects performance measurements and metrics from all parts of the organization. These measurements may be in automated systems on various technical platforms. It takes significant business expertise to understand what is important to collect, and what can remain within the department.

As part of the collection process, certain technologies such as databases and corporate networks need to be understood and leveraged. In the end, all the performance data will be in one place—the CPO needs to begin with this end in mind.

Consolidator

In the role of consolidator, the CPO must take the disjointed performance data and consolidate it into one view. This usually takes the form of a single system or database. This consolidation role will also require significant business knowledge. In particular, expertise in how the measures are used in combination is key. Business expertise and experience will help the CPO decide which data must be homogenized and which can remain distinct. Many parts of the organization will use financial performance measures, but most likely, the measures from the finance organization will serve as the 'data of record.'

One requirement of consolidating performance data is the process of technical consolidation. There are many technical tools and techniques one can use that can assist with technical consolidation such as data warehouses, online analytic processing (OLAP), and data cleansing tools. Ultimately, these systems must remain relevant to the business rules and not just perform technical consolidation of the raw data. This is another area where the risk of chasing 'technical glory' is high. Many technologists will apply pressure to implement more highly automated and highly complex systems than are pragmatically possible, when simple consolidation, using existing technology, is often all that is needed.

The CPO must know when the consolidation can be helped by technology and when the process can be hindered by technology. Since the ultimate goal is to provide a heads-up display for the CEO, pragmatism must rule.

As important a decision as what to consolidate is what not to consolidate. The CPO must use business knowledge and experience to exclude data that should not be consolidated. For example, it may not make sense to consolidate older customer information or long-time discontinued products and their actual order line items. Instead, the CPO may choose to consolidate information about discontinued customers and products to avoid the overhead of processing through thousands of irrelevant line items.

Condenser

The CPO must also play the role of condenser. Even after the performance data has been consolidated, it needs to be condensed into a concentrated form that is usable by executives. The collection and consolidation process may limit, or even filter, some of the data being collected, but in the role of condenser, the CPO must now present the most relevant data. Much of the data collected and consolidated will have too much detail to be usable by the CEO. For example, during collection and consolidation, product level (SKU) information may be used. The CEO, though, will require division level performance data. This not to say that this condensed data should be the only data available, but as condenser of the data, the CPO must present the highest level of data to support the decisions of the CEO. If further data is needed to prove out the higher-level data, that data should be made available as well. As a condenser, the CPO must keep the most relevant data easily accessible without flooding the CEO with unneeded details.

Communicator

The role of communicator is the most important for the CPO. What good is it to have collected, consolidated and condensed the data to only have it locked up in a computer system? Or, worse yet, if it requires an army of dedicated programs to produce 'management reports?' This is actually the downfall of many business intelligence and executive information systems. The CPO must be prepared to communicate the data to the recipient in the most accessible way possible. One size does not fit all. Some executives will only require a Power Point briefing of the most relevant facts supported by some graphs and tables. Others will want a digital dashboard approach of an executive information system, where the executive is able to drill into more detail interactively using a computer system. Others may require detailed briefing books that present an executive summary with supporting analysis results and industry references.

The CPO needs to understand what the executive needs and wants for his or her own version of a heads-up display. Based on these needs, the CPO will need to prepare and present the performance data. As a communicator, the CPO needs to be prepared for two-way communications. The performance data he or she presents will most likely cause the CEO or other executives to take corrective actions. The CPO must be able to understand the actions required and be prepared to explain the results of such an action in terms of performance, while still speaking in executive terms.

Beyond the executive level, the CPO must be able to communicate to upper and middle management their specific interpretation of the performance data. This is not to say that the CPO individually briefs all middle managers. Instead, through his or her technological background, the CPO selects an appropriate delivery mechanism of upper and middle management performance data. This could once again be in the form of briefing books or executive information systems, but it will most likely be in the form of reports and online applications.

In understanding his or her role as communicator, the CPO must be able to apply the proper business filters to the data. Mid-level managers will not be privy to the same data available to the CEO. The CPO communicates at the appropriate level of detail and is always governed by confidentiality parameters set by executive management.

For all the CPO's roles, the performance data is fact-based. Although business experience will guide some of the filtering of data, the CPO can fall into the trap of hunches and intuition. The CPO must remember that he or she is acting as the heads-up display and that the CEO will use their input for making far-reaching decisions. If the CEO solicits an opinion from the CPO, an opinion should be given, but the CPO should never substitute opinion or hunches for facts.

INDUSTRY SPECIFIC OR INDUSTRY NEUTRAL

On the surface, the CPO role seems generic, one that can function the same way in any industry. It is true that every organization in every industry needs a CPO. A question arises, though: does a CPO need to be industry specific?

Comparing their role with other executive level positions lends some insight to this question. The CFO, who is responsible for financial operations, needs to have a strong foundation in finances and the techniques involved. Depending if the organization is growing organically or through mergers and acquisitions, different methods, techniques and skill are needed. Within the CFO field there are certain specialties, such as service organizations, publicly versus privately held, and local versus multi-national reach. All of this will determine what specific skills are needed. Generally, though, CFOs are industry neutral and can move between industries when changing companies.

The CIO or CTO, who is ultimately responsible for technology in an organization, must have a strong technological foundation. Again, depending on the strategy of the organization, different techniques and skills may be required. Some CIO/CTOs will be very skilled in service contracts and outsourcing, while others will be very skilled with in-house development and software package implementations. The CIO/CTO is very much a product of the organization's industry, though. Historically, certain organizations have gravitated towards certain technologies. For example, the insurance industry and public sector have used large mainframe systems and been traditionally aligned with IBM-centric architectures. The financial trading industry has traditionally used high availability and fault-tolerant systems, which use a much different architecture. Hospitality and food services have traditionally been very mid-range centric. Each industry will have its own level of affinity with a certain technology or platform.

This is not to say that a CIO from one of these industries will only have experience in a particular set of technologies, but there is a higher chance of an affinity to certain technologies based on the industry.

If we look at the three required backgrounds of the CPO—business expert, technologist, and interpreter—industry experience does have varying levels of importance. Business experience is the most industry-specific. The interpreter is closely tied to the business expert. A good interpreter is required to have certain vocabulary specific to their industry. Some individuals demonstrate a chameleon-like ability with business vocabulary and terminology, but generally, real business experience rather than buzzword savvy is required. The technologist experience is probably the most industry-transportable. This is further facilitated by standardization and ubiquitous technology trends such as databases, networks, and the Internet. When assessing an industry move, the CPO must take into account the learning curve which he or she will encounter from all three perspectives: business expert, technologist, and interpreter.

MEASURING THE MEASURER

In any role in an organization, measurement of success is critical. There are certain criteria that a CPO must be measured against. The criteria falls into three categories: quality, timeliness and relevancy.

The CPO will be measured on the quality of the performance data he or she presents. It should be obvious that poor data will lead to poor decisions. Similar to the jet fighter, if the heads-up display indicates an altitude of 5000 meters, but the actual altitude is 500 meters, the decisions the pilot makes will be disastrous.

The CPO must ultimately take responsibility for the quality of the performance data being presented. This can put the CPO in a difficult situation: they are held accountable for business data over which they have no control.

A successful CPO will create an environment that is tolerant of poor quality data to a certain degree. This environment will need to detect and compensate for the data deficiencies. There are a number of techniques that can be implemented in areas, such as statistical modeling with confidence ratings, to provide an adequate quality rating of the performance data being presented. The CPO is also measured on his or her ability to point out where the performance data can be improved, even if he or she does not have explicit control over that data. If the fighter pilot notices that the navigation systems are malfunctioning, first he must make immediate adjustments for this deficiency. Upon returning to the hanger, he must let the maintenance crew know what is wrong so it does not continue to be a problem.

Timeliness is the second measurement criterion of the CPO. If the performance data is outdated, can it really be useful in making CEO-level decisions? The CPO needs to have a firm grasp of the importance of timeliness. The CPO must understand the 'shelf life' of the performance data and build adequate refresh strategies. The CPO must also guard against the "I need everything, now" mentality. It is highly unlikely that a CEO will need up-to-the-minute order status with real-time updates to facilitate strategic decisions. A daily, weekly, or even monthly refresh rate may suffice, as long as the proper level of detail is available for confirmation.

Since refreshing the data is typically a resource and information technology intensive process, the CPO must apply the refresh strategy pragmatically to control the cost and overhead. Providing the proper level of timeliness is a key measurement of the CPO.

Combining quality, timeliness and business insight leads to the third measurement of the CPO, relevancy. Much the technology required to provide a heads-up display to the CEO (network, database, application) is readily available, since this is a fairly mature segment of the technology. Implementing the system or technology, though, does not solve the business problem. The CPO must ensure the data is relevant.

Many organizations implemented Executive Information Systems (EIS) in the 80's and 90's. Most of these implementations were technical successes but business failures. Executives were presented with infinite possibilities for analyzing their data. However, most executives do not have infinite time to analyze these infinite possibilities. How many times has the CEO said, "Skip the detail. What is the bottom line?"

The CPO must be able to bring the CEO directly to that 'bottom line.' It is only by providing relevancy that the CPO can do this, not by implementing a computer system mired in detail.

A CPO must be measured against these three criteria: quality, timeliness and relevancy. These three measurement criteria are impacted differently by the four roles (collector, consolidator, condenser, and communicator) of the CPO. As a collector, timeliness becomes the most critical measurement of the CPO. One of the main reasons is that the CPO is performing a balancing act between the timeliness of the data resources and the needs of the CEO. As a consolidator, the CPO is mainly measured in terms of quality. In a consolidation role, there is much correlation and elimination of data, and the CPO must pay particular attention to the garbage-in/garbage-out trap. As a condenser, the CPO is measured against relevancy. With all the data collected and cleansed, the CPO must now use his or her business expertise to condense the data into a relevant package. Finally, as a communicator, the CPO is measured against all three criteria. As a communicator, the CPO must adequately communicate what is in the data, who should be using it, and the applicable time frame in which it should be used.

The CPO is an invaluable role in any organization. By relieving the CEO of having to collect, consolidate, and condense various data related to performance, the CPO acts as a heads-up display for the CEO. The CEO can then concentrate of making the decisions based on performance data. CPOs add value to an organization in four ways:

1. One stop shopping for performance data—The CPO collects and disseminates the disparate performance data spread throughout an organization. With performance data, 'the buck stops here.' The CEO has one place to go for performance management.

2. Accountability—The CPO takes ultimate responsibility for the performance data. Previously, there was not a single point of accountability. This leads to inefficiency and finger pointing.

3. Closing the Loop—The CPO gives an organization the ability to measure their performance, and take action. Since the CPO is presenting this data at an executive level, executives can take actions immediately and the data can then be disseminated to upper and middle management in real time.

4. Decision Enablement—The CPO is ultimately responsible to the CEO, but the data and analysis collected can facilitate decisions at all levels. This can be applied to regional, cost center, product, or

project managers, since they will most likely be the physical implementers of the executive decisions.

Roles of the CPO versus Measures used by the CPO

	Collector	Consolidator	Condenser	Communicator
Quality		X		X
Timeliness	X			X
Relevancy			X	X

Once the CPO is in place, he or she will have to follow a certain methodology in order to fulfill the promise of his role. The next chapter will examine that methodology in terms of its two most critical elements: performance management and scenario-based planning, also known as 'what if' budgeting.

Case Study

A leading global organization in pharmaceuticals and agriculture, employing 95,000 people in more than 120 countries, was created through merger and acquisition activity. Successful integration of this global entity required a high-performance information system that ensured real-time communications between its headquarters and worldwide project management team.

An intranet-based information system, complete with a planning and analysis tool, delivered both quantitative and qualitative information. Now, using a standard Web browser, more than 350 users can administer more than 750 different projects. Positive or negative trends can be quickly identified and acted upon. Plus, the Web-based architecture has saved considerable costs and eliminated the need for "client" installations worldwide. Additional benefits include consistent, worldwide collaborative communications throughout the organization.

2

The CPO's Methodology Explained

A large number of the patents awarded in the United States are not actually for new inventions. Instead, many patents are awarded for unique combinations of existing inventions. For the CEO or the head of any organization, this concept of combining existing practices and technologies should be taken seriously.

Performance management, which provides a holistic view of an organization's performance in both financial and non-financial metrics, is being adopted by many leading organizations. Concurrently, 'what-if' scenario-based planning is extending the applicability and usefulness of budgeting processes to non-financial areas. The unique combination of these two disciplines will enable organizations to react and change faster than industry norms and increase their competitive advantage.

PERFORMANCE MANAGEMENT

Performance management, sometimes referred to as corporate performance management, is an emerging discipline that provides a holistic view of an enterprise. Combining metrics, benchmarks and processes, performance management analyzes financial, as well as non-financial metrics.[1] This combination of metrics offers the complete report card

---

1. Gartner Report SPA-14-9282 12/2001 which states "40% of Global 2000 enterprises will have implemented corporate performance management solutions by 2005 (0.8 probability)

of an enterprise. Often organizations measure themselves purely by financial measurements. Thus, key indicators, such as customer satisfaction, on-time delivery, or employee retention rates are overlooked. This myopic view of financial measurements is often the result of two factors. First, external measurement of an enterprise by investors, analysts, and the markets are almost entirely financial measurements (revenue, margin, etc.). Second, financial measurements are usually readily available from existing systems, such as financial or accounting packages.

Other metrics typically are buried deeper in an organization's systems and processes. These metrics many times are not understood or are represented without empirical backing. Worst of all, these alternate metrics are not usually integrated with the financial metrics.

Data Understanding & Availability

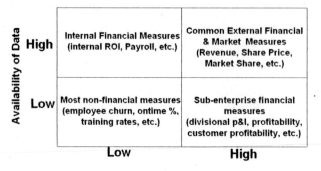

Degree of Universal Understanding of Data

Performance management provides 'one stop shopping' for the metrics by which an enterprise is measured. They are combined in a dashboard-like interface made available to executives and senior management. This is similar to an automobile, in which the dashboard presents a relevant, high-level view of the most vital information, such as speed, fuel level, temperature, and tachometer. Most current performance management systems are disjointed from the actual enterprise resource planning or customer relationship management systems from which they are getting their data. Thus, the technical aspects of creating a performance management system, not only relate to the system itself, but the feeding from these upstream systems.

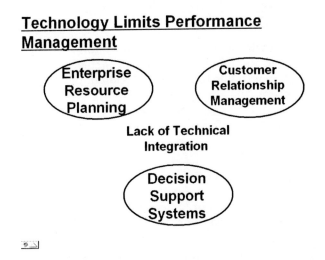

The enterprise that is leveraging performance management can understand that even if financial figures are neutral or positive, other metrics can indicate a less than healthy enterprise.

ASKING "WHAT-IF...?": SCENARIO-BASED PLANNING

Budgeting has traditionally been one of the only forms of metric-based planning an enterprise uses. Most organizations devise a yearly budget and attempt to track actual figures against that budget. These budgets can be highly aggregated at a corporate level and then pushed down to divisions and departments. One organization we work with does exactly this. The centralized finance organization creates a financial budget, mostly consisting of revenue and margin targets, along with variations of these figures. The budgets are completed at a division

level, with some divisions representing hundreds of millions in revenue. At the close of the central budget, the figures are electronically
passed on to each division. It is then at the discretion of each division
to apportion the high-level figure to a department level.

What does Middle Out mean to your organization?

**With Middle Out Planning, organizations
can plan and budget at the level which is
most appropriate to their organization.
For example:**

•**Product**	•**Department**
•**Division**	•**Company**
•**Cost Center**	•**Project**

**The real question is why have
organizations been forced into a choice
between top-down or bottom up, when
Middle Out is really what they need?**

A new trend, which has only recently been enabled by technology is
scenario-based planning. Until recently, organizations barely had the
time to create a budget and make minor adjustments to it. Now, with
new technology that enables combinations of top-down, bottom-up,
and middle-out planning, enterprises have the ability to perform more
'what-if' scenario planning.

With this methodology, organizations usually create a baseline budget. This baseline is then used to generate multiple, and sometimes
hundreds, of scenarios. By utilizing top-down budgeting that enables
'splashing', or automated apportionment, of data, enterprises can now
create these 'what-if' scenarios. With splashing, if numbers are entered
at a mid-level, such as the product line or cost center, the numbers
below are automatically populated based on business rules. In the case
of products lines, the numbers would be populated down to an SKU
level. In this sense, the data is splashed downward, similar to a water-

fall. For example, one organization creates a top-line revenue target. The budget is then shared with product-line managers, who are responsible for dozens of products. The product-line manager can then adjust their target for each product or adjust their overall product target. With each change, the top line numbers are being changed. The same budget is shared with regional sales managers. They can adjust their targets for sales representatives and the data is also automatically aggregated. The sum of these changes is recorded as a scenario and the process is repeated. It is this collaborative processing between all parts of an enterprise that facilitates the time compression to allow multiple scenario building.

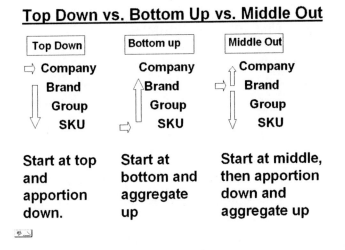

Top Down vs. Bottom Up vs. Middle Out

Top Down	Bottom up	Middle Out
Company	Company	Company
Brand	Brand	Brand
Group	Group	Group
SKU	SKU	SKU
Start at top and apportion down.	Start at bottom and aggregate up	Start at middle, then apportion down and aggregate up

Another emerging trend in planning has been the integration of non-financial metrics into the planning process. By understanding the trends of past metrics, such as employee attrition, on-time delivery rate, or average lead-time for new products, forward-looking forecasts can be derived. The same method of 'splashing' also allows multiple scenario building. Although only a few organizations are performing this forecast, even less are integrating it into their other metrics, in particular, financial metrics.

Examples of Middle Out

Starting Point:	Aggregates to:	Apportions to:
Brand Manager	Division or Company	SKUs or Products
Branch Manager	State, Region or Country	Sales Reps or Territory
R&D Project Manager	Programs or Initiatives	Tasks or Phases
Division VP	Company or Enterprise	Brands, Regions, Cost Centers

PERFORMANCE MANAGEMENT OPTIMIZATION

A few leading organizations are now combining performance management and scenario-based planning. This new discipline applies the metric measurement across multiple functions in a business to not only the actual data, but also the what-if scenarios.

This bridges a serious gap that exists between performance management and what-if scenario planning. Until recently, performance management has been focused solely on history. Organizations can see at a certain point in time how they have performed up until that day, but looking forward was not an option.

Performance optimization management (POM) combines performance management of the possible business scenarios in order to find the optimal solution. This is achieved in a three-step process:

1. Use the disciplines and tools of performance management to understand the 'as-is,' today. This static snapshot serves as a baseline to future scenarios.

2. Using what-if scenario planning tools, create dozens of scenarios for the best and worst cases. There can be simultaneous adjust-

ments to multiple view of the business. For example, the product managers can update their what-if measures while research & development update theirs against the same model. The what-if scenarios are for financial and non-financial metrics. A centralized group keeps versions of these scenarios for later analysis.

Concurrently, performance management is being done against the what-if scenarios. By measuring these possible future states, strengths and weaknesses can be determined before any physical changes are invoked. Besides measuring each scenario individually, cross-scenario measurements are analyzed to determine if a hybrid of two scenarios may be optimal.

3. An optimal scenario is selected by the organization. Optimal needs to be based on not only the financial measure, but also the non-financial measures. Thus, the optimal solution may not always be the solution with the highest revenue or margin (although these measures typically are weighted more heavily). For example, an optimal scenario for revenue may be a dismal scenario for projected customer churn.

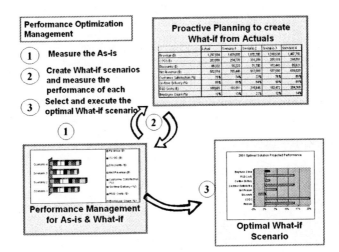

INTERNAL AND EXTERNAL FOCUS

Many organizations regard performance management and optimization as internally focused. These organizations will focus on their own financial and non-financial measures. The data and processes will be very internally focused. Existing ERP systems and CRM systems will be the basis for much of the raw information needed for this. The main focus is to fix the organization from within. Other organizations will need to look outside of their organization to obtain the raw data and measures needed for a complete view.

INTERNAL FOCUS

By concentrating on their area of influence, specifically their wholly owned processes and data, organizations can achieve accelerated benefits of POM. This is possible through two main influencing factors. First, the data is usually readily available from existing internal systems. There may still be a question of the quality and usability of the data that will be open, but regardless, the data in its raw form should be available. Second, the processes are usually better understood from an internal perspective. Organizations usually have been utilizing internal processes and have engrained them into the fabric of the organization. Thus, understanding how the raw data was created should be obtainable information.

This internal focus, though providing accelerated benefits, usually will not provide a complete view of an organization. Global supply chains, business partnerships, outsourced relationships and changing corporate structures have driven the need for an external as well as internal focus for POM.

EXTERNAL FOCUS

External focus adds a new set of challenges, that may not only be difficult to implement, but many times difficult to understand. Generally, the processes and data outside an organization will not follow the same structure, documentations and standards as internal processes. Take, for example, an organization that has outsourced the delivery of end products via a third-party logistics company. While much may be understood regarding the products being developed and produced, including common naming and product codes, this level of data may not be available from outside systems. A third-party company may just be able to track batches or distributions of products, and will not be able to link products to customer sales, which is possible through internal systems.

This challenge, though, is not insurmountable. If business partners are truly partners, their information technology staff will be able to properly communicate the structure and content of the needed data. There are a number of emerging technology standards, based on Internet protocols, to facilitate this sharing of data. Organizations that do not recognize and take advantage of standards may not have the best interest of their business partners in mind by taking a short-term focus on technology. Many times, not adhering to standards represents the easy or inexpensive technical solution. With greater interdependence between business partners, the technological chain is only as strong as the weakest link.

COMBINING EXTERNAL AND INTERNAL FOCUS

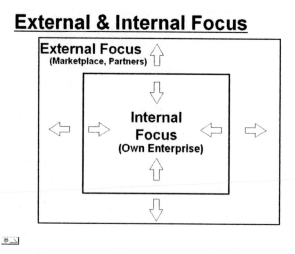

An organization that combines the external and internal focus will have a complete end-to-end ability to leverage POM. Many organizations will start with the internal focus to not only test the POM methodology, but also to provide early return on investment (ROI). Once the business benefit is achieved from internal focus, external focus then augments the process.

A POM-enabled organization must build a framework and technical architecture that does not hard-wire the organization to any internal or external systems. It is almost certain that one or more of these systems will be retired, swapped or upgraded within a two-year period. POM implementations must be flexible enough to avoid being at the mercy of technical limitations and upgrades. Thus, the framework must be built for business measures, not technical fields or jargon.

THE NETWORKED POM ENVIRONMENT

Networked POM

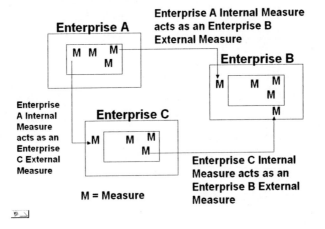

Enterprise A Internal Measure acts as an Enterprise B External Measure

Enterprise A

Enterprise B

Enterprise A Internal Measure acts as an Enterprise C External Measure

Enterprise C

Enterprise C Internal Measure acts as an Enterprise B External Measure

M = Measure

In a truly networked POM environment, the internal focus of one organization will be the external focus of a business partner. If organizations can leverage the networked POM environment, they will be able to manage performance with less effort than the solely internally focused organization. Much of the workload for creating the complete view of the performance of an organization is shared by business partners. With this shared responsibility, comes shared rewards. Networked POM environments are two-way information sharing organizations. In the outsourced logistics example, the logistics company has certain KPIs, such as on-time delivery, average lead-time, empty container percentage, etc. If these measures are managed as internally focused POM indicators, they can then be shared with the product manufacturer for integration as external focus measures for their POM system. It is this two-way sharing of measures that will benefit both business partners.

One caveat in the networked POM environment, though, is data security and privacy. An outsourcer, such as the logistics company, may perform services for competing companies. This data could be used to learn the strong and weak points of their competitions, thus providing a competitive advantage. Proper safeguards must take into account not only the security issue of the individual data, but also the privacy of the combined data. Interestingly, the data from one company becomes even more valuable to competitors when compared to other companies. Thus, by examining the individual data from companies along with the combined or aggregated data, strong and weak points relative to the market can be derived.

The safeguard of the data can be obtained technically through existing technologies, such as segmentation of servers and firewalls. Technical safeguards need to be complemented by process safeguards include policies, procedures and audits.

SUCCESS FACTORS OF POM

The POM Formula

Internal Measures Company A

$$+ \quad \frac{\text{External Measures}_{\text{Relevant to Company A}}}{\text{Performance Measures}_{\text{Company A}}}$$

With this combination of the disciplines of performance management and scenario-based planning, there are five technical critical success factors. Without applying all five, the POM methodology will be difficult, if not impossible to implement.

Usability

A successful implementation of POM will build on the successful budgeting systems of today. With a vast majority of financial users budgeting and planning in Microsoft Excel, it is the logical platform of choice. The increased functionality of pivot tables and multidimensional views are becoming more commonplace.

Additionally, technologies from industry leads such as Microsoft provide a built-in multidimensional engine. This engine combined with a write-back enabled, spreadsheet-based front end will allow the flexibility to build the 'what-if' scenarios required in POM.

Splashing

Splashing is the ability to enter data at any level of aggregation (cost center, product line, division, etc.) and have the data apportioned based on patterns or business rules. Concurrently, the 'top-line' rollup is also updated. This gives the user true 'middle-out' planning capabilities. Much of the current technology can aggregate up when low level figures are entered, fewer can apportion down, and even fewer can combine both.

Data Proliferation without Splashing

Assume: 100 Products
50 Sales Regions
200 Distribution Channels
750 Time Periods (Days)
10,000 Customers

Total Data Points
$$=100 * 50 * 200 * 750 * 10,000$$
$$= 7,300,000,000,000$$
(7.3 Trillion)

Splashing must have multiple methods. First, even distribution will splash the aggregated number over all the elements below it at equal levels. Second, percent changes can be combined with the even distribution. Thus, a divisional number could be evenly spread out among departments, but with each individual number increased by 10%. Third, and more complex, distribution can be contoured.

Controlled Data with Splashing

Assume: 100 Products
50 Sales Regions
200 Distribution Channels
750 Time Periods (Days)
10,000 Customers

If we enter at the Region, Month, Level we only enter 50 * 12 = 600 values, but we will yield the same 7.3 Trillion apportioned data points.

With contouring, a number is entered at an aggregated level, but is splashed based on a second set of numbers. Thus, a department could enter a forecast number for revenue target, but splash based on last year's product distribution.

<u>Determining a Splash Ratio</u>

Total # of Values Populated
Total # of Values Entered

In our previous case we had $\dfrac{\textbf{7.3 Trillion}}{\textbf{600}}$

A true splashing environment combines all three forms in a work-flow that leverages the concurrency of decentralized planning, while retaining control of centralized functions. For example, a tire manufacturing company can allow country sales managers to forecast revenue. Using contour distribution splashing, distribution within that country of product revenue can be automatically generated based on past performance. Concurrently, product managers can update their cost projections and perform percent increases based on expected increased cost of raw materials. When completed, a central planning group can then fine tune the top-line numbers and splash accordingly.

Integration of Non-Financial Measures

Many systems can measure financial information, such as revenue, profit, and cost of goods. Some of these systems also have the capability to perform activity-based costing. Generally, though, organizations need to have a separate system for other types of performance such as manufacturing, human resources, or supply chain. POM can only deliver its greatest return on investment when all these measures are integrated into one application.

Savvy organizations can perform this task with a group of programmers, creating custom code and reports, but the total cost of ownership is unjustifiable. Even with these homegrown systems, the ability to perform what-if scenarios against all measures is lacking.

Non Financial Measures Examples

Measure	Source
Customer Satisfaction Level	CRM or Call Center
On-Time Delivery	ERP
Employee Churn %	HR or ERP System
Project Turnaround Time	R&D or Project Reporting Systems

Historical data is one of the major components of forecasting scenarios for future business. With historical data, the ability to forecast future data becomes easier. This is not just true for financial data, but also non-financial. For example, an organization may use past on-time delivery percentages to forecast next year's expected percentage. Also, the organization can modify certain constraints and variables to determine a new forecast for the on-time delivery percentage. This process is actually quite similar to forecasting financial values.

Forward and Historical Views

Many current performance management implementations are strictly limited to the historical data. Although business value can be derived from knowing where you have been, greater value lies in knowing where you will go. Interestingly enough, many of the basic principles and technology of the historical performance management methods are applicable to forward oriented performance management.

A key part missing in most implementations is optimization. By generating multiple what-if scenarios and applying performance management as if in actual situations, performance management is taken to the next level. Through an iterative process of generating scenarios and measuring the expected performance, an optimal balanced outcome can be selected.

ABILITY TO ACT

A widely known shortcoming of any business intelligence application is the separation of analytical and actionable processes. Even with the best analytical system, if there is not the ability to translate this automatically into an actionable process, such as a complete budget or business plan, the analytics become nothing more than more fancy and complex reporting.

It is the 'write-back' capability that so many business intelligence vendors have distanced themselves from. Write-back allows actions to be taken immediately by the user of the system. If sales numbers seem soft, the user can create a scenario for stronger numbers and examine the results immediately. Unnatural separation of analytical and actionable processes, by separating write-back operations, creates disconnects between the business process and the technical implementation. Disconnects of this level lead to double work, in the form of data entry, and are prone to error, just like any double entry. The separation also robs the organization of valuable time that could be spent optimizing, but is instead wasted on double entry and data checking.

An optimal solution would allow the optimal what-if scenario to be integrated with the traditional budgeting and planning system, allowing for seamless transition from optimization to actionable processes.

COLLABORATION AND DISTRIBUTION

Technology has made collaboration possible for budgeting. Although many organizations do not take advantage of this technology yet, the ability exists to perform combined decentralized (sales field office, divisional, etc.) and centralized (home office, consolidated financial) budgeting. During this process organizations use collaborative technologies such as intranets and shared databases to facilitate information sharing in real time.

This same process needs to be applied to scenario-based planning. Organizations can take advantage of the decentralized facilities to perform what-if plans on a field office or product-line level. Concurrently, enterprise level assumptions can be applied to the same what-if scenarios by a centralized organization.

Key to the success is the planning of both financial and non-financial measures. For example, a sales manager in a Latin American subsidiary could plan for increased customer satisfaction by adding a local language help desk. This would be offset by the increased overhead for the Latin American office. The corporate office in California can estimate the cost of rerouting all Spanish-speaking help desk calls to the new call center and examine economies of scale. This results in a collaboration of decentralized scenarios with centralized sharing control.

Technology must also be used for distribution of the information. Business users need the ability to view and manipulate in their technology of choice. Many analysts are used to Microsoft Excel and would rather stay in that environment instead of learning the latest web based technology. Alternatively, for cost efficient distribution of the results and reports, the intranet is key. Lastly, on the executive level, a briefing book that contains the key information needed on the C-level, in a concise easy to read business document or presentation, is key.

The optimal POM environment will allow collaboration and distribution at all levels and through various technologies without requiring custom code or third party add-ons.

Five Success Factors of POM

1. Usability
2. Splashing
3. Integration of Non-Financial Measures
4. Forward & Historical Views
5. Ability to Act

Organizations can achieve significant competitive advantage through the use of performance management optimization. The two disciplines of performance management and scenario-based planning can be intertwined, creating an environment where not only the actual as-is state is measured, but the optimal what-if scenario is achieved.

The following three chapters of this book will examine the new environment in which the CPO must function. It is an environment of fast-paced change—change that must be managed efficiently and in real time.

Case Study

An information storage solutions provider with annual sales in excess of $2 billion has more than 8,500 employees in 60 countries worldwide. Frustrated by restrictions in software that held them back from reporting in the manner they needed to, they evaluated a number of products. After selecting and implementing a corporate forecasting product from a big ERP vendor, they were ready to give up in total frustration because it was slow, difficult to use, and undependable.

To avoid having the same issues again, they purchased a business intelligence suite for use as a management reporting system. Data was extracted from the corporate forecasting system into the suite and suddenly, the storage solutions provider was able to report hours, sometimes days ahead of those that were still using the existing system. It's no surprise that the suite became the company's forecasting and analysis software worldwide. The software is very much in demand by financial as well as non-financial users.

3

Harnessing the Velocity of Change

Pose this question to your CEO: "Has our organization implemented any business intelligence systems that gives us a competitive advantage?" Unless your organization is the exception, the answer will be either "No" or "Such as…?"

The reality is that business intelligence (BI) has not had the impact on the bottom line that has been promised by the industry. It seems like there is a lot of movement from red squares to black squares, but nobody is really playing the game. If you are the CEO, or even a regular shareholder, you should be infuriated by the lack of business value from such large investments.

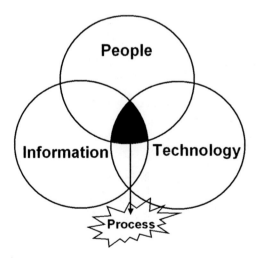

Digging deeper, some interesting conclusions can be drawn. Despite all the data-centric techniques in business intelligence, the key is really the process. There are three major building blocks of any system, even non-computerized systems: people, disciplines, and information. The people form the core of any organization, along with the organizational structure. Disciplines are the actions of the people; for example, a CFO may use the discipline of financial forecasting, while a research and development group may use the discipline of quality assurance. Information can be in automated or non-automated systems. It is the intersection of the people, information and discipline that defines the process. The process is the glue that holds this structure together.

Business practices of the past called for more of a mono-dimensional, symmetrical approach. The business could be managed around a known environment and predictable time frames. Predictability was high, processes were static, and planning horizons were far-reaching.

Globalization moves companies from mono dimensional to multi dimensional process oriented organizations

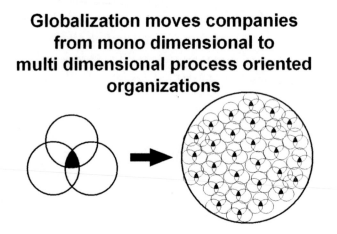

Globalization and other external forces, though, have forced companies to move from a mono-dimensional approach to a multidimensional approach to managing the business. Consequently, the processes have become more asymmetrical.

Using e-business as an example, an organization may have a multi-process environment that they are trying to manage and contain through internal controls. Although there are many processes, they are able to contain them with some form of controlling mechanism (such as a financial reporting system or a consolidated budget). E-business is then introduced and changes everything, including the rules of the game. The velocity of change is greatly accelerated. Decisions need to be made in Internet time, while business models become more disparate.

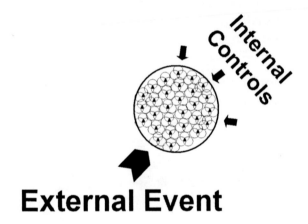

External Event

These two changes act as a centrifugal force that diminishes control over the core processes of the business. The higher the velocity or greater the disparity, the greater the force. Organizations that cannot harness the power of this trend will be crushed by it.

E-business is used here as an example. Just as easily, a down-turning economic environment or changing regulation or competitive pressures can have the same effect.

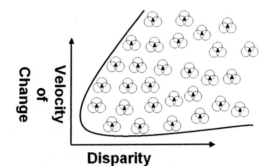

Disparity

Decision-process velocity and growing organization complexity act as centrifugal forces that paralyze the decision process.

Caught in this whirlwind of change, many organizations try the traditional BI approach, turning to their stand-alone systems, such as a sales reporting system, budgeting application, or data warehouse. They might even turn to a transactional reporting system, but these are limited in their effectiveness and scope due to their stovepipe nature.

Many organizations have built specific applications and business intelligence systems to support these pockets of process, yet they have not been able to harness the power of change. Faster stovepipes, though, are not the solution. The systems are not able to react at the speed which business demands, rendering the stovepipe systems useless.

The velocity of change and disparate business environments are creating the need for an environment that enables all critical business processes to be supported together. Savvy businesses (and e-businesses alike) rely on Collaborative Analytical Processing (CAP) to centrally manage BI functions. The linear approach is no longer sufficient. Key cross-functional areas are critical, including:

End user modeling, which allows users to make changes to business models in real time directly in the same environment used for browsing and entering data.

Collaborative modeling, which allows teams to work on one application together on a role-based model without sacrificing security or control.

Waterfall modeling, which allows structured modeling workflows in the company, giving each department the freedom to extend centrally defined structures by their individual business needs.

Perpetually changing applications, which are capable of handling dynamic changes from day to day, department-to-department, and process-to-process as in real business.

Integration of content and workflow, which enriches analytical applications with any type of content that helps to increase understanding of the business.

Without each of the components of CAP, organizations will be crushed by the velocity of change, while organizations that embrace CAP will harness the velocity of change. Continuous business planning and shared access to information (and its analysis) makes CAP a smart, cost-effective tool when used correctly. Having open standards is critical to its success.

BI has matured as a technology practice. No longer should it be acceptable to start with a blank screen. How many ways can a company do budgeting or click stream analysis, really? The key though is what to do beyond the common functions. By utilizing templates and applications, organizations can concentrate on the value-add instead of the 'me too.'

CAP[1] represents a unique approach when compared to the traditional brute force method of so many failed projects. Interestingly, though, the European market has seen great success with this process-centric, finessed approach. It's now up to the U.S. to repeat this success.

Can we do it? Certainly. But we need to open ourselves up to new ways of thinking about change and its management. Contrary to popular belief, "change" and "management" need not be mutually exclusive terms. Along those lines, in the next chapter, we'll look at a key concept in the next wave of business intelligence: Managing the Delta.

Case Study

A U.S. based subsidiary of a German-based company offers anesthesia, critical care and information systems to meet the needs of today's hospitals. The ability to quickly and easily monitor business results and forecast news expectations was crucial, especially through one single user-friendly interface. After weighing its options, the company selected a powerful integrated suite of solutions for budgeting, reporting, consolidation, and analysis. It provides automation and scheduling of enterprise data directly from existing tables to ensure integrity of data and reporting. It also provides real-time dynamic rolls ups and assessments and conducts assumption analysis.

The result is a fully automated and integrated intelligence framework to support future growth. Seeing trends in data to assess variances–graphically depicted–means the organization can provide continual forecast management.

---

1.   "CAP was originally conceived and introduced by MIS AG, Darmstadt, Germany in January 2000."

4

Managing the Delta by Watching the Dashboard

Imagine you are driving your car down the freeway at sixty miles per hour. There are various gauges and circumstantial inputs that are guiding your immediate decisions. Do I speed up? Is there a hazard in my lane? Do I change lanes? Do I need gas? There are, though, a number of factors that are not components of these decisions, such as the weight of your car, its color, its tire size, the number of passengers it can carry, and so on. Although these considerations were important factors in your selection of your car and in its long-term management, they are not impacting the management of the moment, i.e., of what is changing and what can be controlled.

Delta (n)

del•ta

1 : the 4th letter of the Greek alphabet -- see ALPHABET table

2 : something shaped like a capital Greek delta; especially : the alluvial deposit at the mouth of a river

3 : an increment of a variable -- symbol Δ :

Source: Merriam-Webster Dictionary

Now, take yourself out of the car driver's seat and place yourself in the CEO chair. Your business is moving along, changing, reacting and growing. Your gauges are the Key Performance Indicators (KPIs). What are my sales? How is this quarter's profitability? What is the status of the new product in the pipeline? What is my customer churn rate? As the CEO, you are managing what can be measured and what can be changed. This is the very essence of Managing the Delta, or managing the change.

Similar to the car driver, the CEO has limited resources to dedicate to gathering these KPIs and applying action. Also similarly, the CEO needs to manage what is changing and what can be controlled. In the past this was not possible because of a lack of data. Ironically, now it is difficult because of a glut of data. With all the data from the enterprise resource planning (ERP) systems, customer relationship management (CRM) systems, external market data, competitive intelligence, and the various legacy systems, the process of getting to the KPIs is often insurmountable. CEOs are forced to make decisions without solid metrics.

Managing the Delta is more a process enabled by technology than a technical system. There has been much talk about executive information systems and dashboards over the past decade, but much of this has been either hype or so mired in technical details that it is limited to the IT professionals.

Characteristics of Managing the Delta are: 1) Cohesion of Metrics, Time Series and Variances, 2) Leveraging historical data, 3) Masking the technology.

Metrics, Time Series & Variances

The very basis of managing the Delta is that something needs to be measured. Are we measuring revenue, profitability, new product progress, customer or employee churn rates? The metrics are the KPIs. Basically, they are the answer to the simple question "How are we doing?" Most C-level (CEO, CFO, etc.) executives will answer this question with a set of KPIs (sales are up 20% this quarter, our customer churn rates are down 4% compared to last month, our profitability is up 7% compared to this quarter last year).

Metrics are not alone in their relevance. Every organization measures against time. Whether it is quarters, days, year-to-date, or months, it is time that provides context to the indicator. It is not enough to say, "Sales are up twenty percent." Twenty percent compared to what? Last quarter? Last month? Metrics must be combined with a time frame to provide a complete picture.

Although, absolute measurements are important, managing the Delta is looking at what is changing and what can be controlled. Knowing that sales were $40 million this month does help, but what are they compared to last month, or this month last year? "Sales were up $8 million to $40 million this month compared to the same month last year" is the exact type of statement that satisfies metrics, variances and time series.

Leveraging Historical Data

KPIs require historical data from some system. It is this history that provides a baseline for the time-based measurement. Most historical data is locked in an ERP, CRM, external system, or legacy system. If an organization is lucky, they have built a data warehouse and have some of this data consolidated already. As any statistics book will state, the larger the sample size, or amount of data, the greater the confidence rating. Organizations that have rich amounts of data have a head start on organizations that have only short-term data.

Sources of Historical Data

1. Enterprise Resource Planning (ERP)
2. Customer Relationship Management (CRM)
3. Sales Force Automation (SFA)
4. Legacy Systems (Mainframe, midrange)
5. Disparate Systems (Spreadsheets, personal databases)

It is not enough to have the historical data, though. The data must also be available. Many organizations have years of historical data, but it is locked into a proprietary format or database. These organizations are first forced to extract this data from the proprietary systems and put them into a standard database such as Microsoft SQL Server or Oracle. This effort is not trivial and typically involves complex information technology processes. Adding to the complexity is the questionable quality of this older proprietary data. More often than not, this older data needs to be cleansed, through a complex IT process known as Extraction, Transformation and Loading (ETL). So complex is this process that a whole sub-industry has been built around ETL.

The Growth of ETL

Extraction, Transformation and Loading (ETL) started with simple programs to move files and data. In the late 1990's with the explosion of the data warehousing market, ETL grew into a complex systems that only a handful of people in an organization can understand.
Thus, by trying to alleviate data backlogs and building a data warehouse, many organizations have created a new backlog, the knowledge locked up in the ETL tool.

If, though, an organization can overcome the consolidation and cleansing of the data, they can then harvest the historical data. Organizations have also questioned whether this ETL process was an all or nothing proposition. An organization can still get the benefits of managing the Delta with only some of the data. If, for example, an organization, has implemented a new CRM system, such as Siebel or Oracle, but their supply chain data is locked up in a proprietary home grown system, they can still apply Delta Management to the CRM-related KPIs. If eventually, an organization does implement a new ERP system such as SAP, the data can then be integrated to provide more robust, CEO-level KPIs.

It is in building this 'federated' approach that forethought is key. Such industry experts as Doug Hackney and Tom Brackett have written numerous books and articles on this subject. Following one of these 'federated' approaches is critical to any organization's long term IT management strategy.

Masking the Technology

End-users need to be sheltered from the inner workings of the technology and concentrate on the business. A few years ago, I worked with an organization that had attempted to build a data mart for sales. Although the project hit some technical snags that were overcome with some ingenuity and a lot of money, the overall failure of the initial project was due to technical saturation. This organization had not only tried to bring the group from paper-based mainframe reports to OLAP, but they also decided to educate over 400 field people in star schemas, dimensions and other technicalities. This is what caused the initial failure of this project.

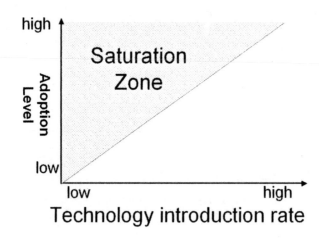

Instead of hiding the inner workings and nuances of the application from the end users, the IT organization instead chose to educate field sales people in IT disciplines. In order to recover from this misstep, the next release of this system was actually a step back in technology. Instead of users picking dimensions, measures and cross drilling, a set of guided KPI reports were placed in an easy-to-use Web interface that sheltered the users from the technicalities. Lesson learned: avoid technical saturation of the user base.

By masking the technology, a true KPI management application can be on the desktop of high-level managers and executives without the need for a dedicated interpreter from the IT department.

Technical Overload

Most technologies take months from introduction to be adopted at a business process level. Yet, many IT organizations are introducing new technologies before the previous wave can be understood and integrated with the business process. Business users quickly become overloaded, or technically saturated. Thus the productivity gains promised and expected from new technologies are lost.

In another organization involved in complex direct marketing, there was a small group of statistically savvy people who worked with an advanced statistical tool. This group was responsible for creating reports based on these advanced tools. The major problem was in the bottleneck created by this organization. The small organization, which represented less than one percent of the staff, was responsible for the data which most of the organization relied on for strategic and tactical decisions.

ARCHITECTURE OF A DELTA MANAGEMENT TOOLSET

A toolset that enables one to manage the Delta uses a set of existing technologies in combination with a process-centric approach. Delta Management uses a two-step approach to analyzing the data, known as Delta Mining. In addition, advanced statistical modeling techniques are built in for non-statisticians to use. All this needs to be wrapped in an intuitive, dashboard-like visual interface.

Delta Mining

Many trade magazines have mentioned data mining as a new wave of data analysis. Although data mining does represent vast increases in the way data can be analyzed, it is mired in technical sophistication that most organizations cannot handle. Data mining is very good at discovering trends and anomalies in the data by examining very large sets of historical data. This data is usually loaded into a proprietary data-mining database built specifically for the algorithm contained in the data-mining tool.

Despite all its advanced features, data mining has never caught on the way it was originally expected to. One can hypothesize that data mining carries a stigma similar to artificial intelligence: great academic theory with horrible practical application.

Delta Mining, although based on data mining, is quite different. While data mining examines large amounts of data, much of the time and computer resources are spent on the large amounts of data. Basically, the program is spending large amounts of resources to pass through the data a few times. From these few passes, trends or anomalies can be detected and presented to the user of the system.

Delta Mining is a two-step approach. First, the data set is examined for static or irrelevant data. This data is then eliminated from the analysis. Second, the analysis concentrates on the changing data, or the Delta. In Delta Mining, more resources are spent doing more detailed analysis on the small amount of relevant data.

This amounts to high confidence ratings even when using very large data sets, through which data mining tools may have managed only a few passes. For example, assume that there is a data set with 1000 different data points (sales orders, customer interactions, supply actions, etc.). Next, assume that there are only 1000 units of computing resource (whether instructions, cycles or any other measure) that the computer can spend on examining this data. This results in a 1:1 ratio of resources to data points, or one pass through the data-mining algorithm.

The Delta Mining scenario yields a very different result. Take the same assumptions of 1000 data points and 1000 units of computing resource. Add to this now that of the 1000 data points, only 20 percent have changed, while 80 percent remain static. This yields 200 data points for 1000 units of computing, or a 5:1 ratio of resources to data point. In this example, the system can spend five times as much effort on the most relevant data. Statistically, this should increase the confidence rating and enable a more metric-based approach to decision making.

Advanced Statistical Modeling & Visual Interface

Now that the relevant data set has been reduced, resulting in more resources per data point, advanced statistical modeling needs to be employed. This advanced modeling, though, needs to be employed behind the scenes. The user should not have to open a statistics book from college to understand r-values and standard deviations. Instead, complex functions like time series analysis or affinity analysis need to be presented in a wizard-driven approach that uses the functions, but does not require detailed statistical knowledge by the user.

The actual user interface needs to be dashboard-like in nature. The most relevant delta values need to be presented in both graphical and tabular format. Additionally, a tree of analysis, or a history of what analysis has been applied should also be part of the dashboard.

Case Study:

A global developer and distributor of household and commercial water filtration systems needed to unify its budgeting, reporting and business analysis functions. With almost 800 employees in multiple locations, the company wanted to consolidate actual and budget data from local offices with corporate data.

To ensure optimal performance, the company implemented an integrated system that supports a variety of functions, such as management accounting, marginal costing, and market analysis. Now they can gain a crisp view of product lifecycles through historical data, determine margin costs and use monthly rolling forecasts to adjust production in a timely manner–all from one dashboard!

Three-level Example

Let us look at managing the Delta through three separate examples. Imagine there are three separate companies with differing levels of maturity in Delta Management. Company A does not have any real decision support systems. They manage their analytical data through a set of static reports delivered via paper and the company's intranet. Company B has completed a Web-enabled OLAP system using one of the leading technology vendors in this space. They have the ability to drill-up, drill-down, drill-across, and create ad-hoc reports. Company C has enabled Delta Mining and has put a Delta Mining dashboard on the desk of key decision makers. In all cases the assumption is that there are 1000 data points and 1000 available computing resource units (MIPS, cycles, dollars). Each company would have a much different approach to understanding and reacting to changes in their business, based on the constraints placed on their data analysis capabilities. Although there is no way to determine if Company A, B or C would make the proper business decision based on Table 1, it is clear that Company C is at an advantage when making metric-based decisions.

For the most part, companies have been trapped into a technological paradigm that does not allow them to manage the Delta. Because of past limitations in technology and usability, organizations have been forced to rely on either non metric-based decisions or place their decision support capabilities in the hands of a select few statistically inclined individuals. This has limited key decision makers in managing what is changing and what can be controlled.

Happily, advances in decision support systems have now enabled organizations to comfortably manage the Delta and concentrate on optimizing what can be controlled. This change, though, is not primarily a technological change, although technology is its enabler. The real change lies in how decisions are made and in how computing resources are deployed against the most relevant of data. Data is no longer heaped together and siphoned through in the hopes of finding the needle in the haystack.

Although, this is major step for most organizations, it is probably a more natural and intuitive way to manage business. Just as in real-life situations, business in managed in the delta, or in what is changing. Organizations that can harness this change can make better informed, metrics-based decisions. Moreover, as the next chapter will demonstrate, they can do so with significant reduction in the time it takes to make those decisions, especially in the financial realm.

Table 1

	Company A	Company B	Company C
Decision Support Delivery Method	Static Reports	Drillable Reports	Delta Management Dashboard
Data Analysis Mode	Gather as much data as possible in attempt to make some sense of past patterns.	Hunt and peck through online reports to find an anomaly or trend.	Examine and act upon changes in the relevant data.
Data Set for Analysis	Some data, if it is in a data warehouse. If not, try to correlate various manual sources.	One data set containing all data, both relevant and irrelevant.	Data is separated into relevant and irrelevant with analysis taking place on only relevant changing data.
Computing Resource to Data Point ratio	Very low, if present at all.	1:1 at best.	High. Directly proportional to amount of relevant data discovered.

Table 1 **(Continued)**

Type of Technology employed	Manual reports against transaction systems such as SAP, PeopleSoft, or Oracle.	Data Warehouses, Data Marts, Data Mining	Data Warehouse combined with Delta Mining
Percentage of users in organization enabled for high power analysis	Little or none. Due to lack of consolidated data or tools.	Low. Generally less than 2% because of the learning curve of high-end tools and data mining.	Medium—High. Up to 50% of an organization can be empowered through Delta Mining and a dashboard interface to the data.

5

Real Time Data for Real Time Decisions

Many organizations are faced with making serious far-reaching financial decisions without having current, accurate data to support them. Financial organizations typically spend an abundance of time and effort to perform tasks such as monthly, quarterly, and year-end closing. This leaves little or no time for strategic planning based on these actual figures. If an organization could minimize the time and effort required to consolidate financial figures and close the books, they could spend more time making informed, metrics-based decisions with real-time data.

Organizations often make far-reaching business decisions based on hunches, assumptions, or guesses. If, however, organizations were provided with benchmarks, their hunches could be empirically tested.

Unless an organization can accumulate or acquire meaningful benchmarks, actual performance cannot be measured. Any organization can measure productivity in terms of units per hour or turnaround time, but performance measurement is multifaceted, and ties this in with benchmarks.

Matching data needs and timeliness

	Real time	Historical
Aggregated	Tactical & Divisional	Strategic
Detailed	Production	Quality Assurance

Data Need (left axis: Aggregated / Detailed)

Real time   Historical

Data Timeliness

In addition to lacking sufficient time, most organizations also lack the tools and the appropriate process for effective performance measurement and management. So much technology has been focused on automation and operational issues, such as ERP, that the tools required to leverage this investment have been left out or underutilized. Even if the technology and processes are in place, the quality of the data can impact performance management. If an organization uses industry benchmarks, but their own data is suspect, the ultimate measurement of performance will also be suspect.

This touches again on timeliness. If the data is not current and we are constantly measuring only the past, stale data, organizations will not be able to break free of this constant catching up game. In turn, this touches on closed-loop decision support. Not only should we be able to measure the performance, but also we should be able to tie in actionable items. If an organization knows they are losing market share or key customers, they should be able to take this information as a basis for a new plan and act on it directly.

At this point, each department's performance can be measured. For example:

- Accounts Receivable Department: Are all invoices generated accurately? Were all credits given to the appropriate customers? Both tasks can influence inventory counts. Revenue levels thus affect the net profit.

- Accounts Payable Department: Are all vendor invoices coded to the General Ledger account? Are all vendor invoices entered up to date? Both tasks influence inventory, expenses, and net profit.

- Credit Department: Does the credit manager have the tools to calculate the DSO (Day Sales Outstanding) during the month in order to contact late paying customers, thus improving the DSO at month's end? The DSO is the usual performance benchmark against which a credit manager is measured. If he or she has the real-time tools to act during the month, then he or she can positively influence the outcome of his performance at month's end. Bringing more cash in faster means paying the short-term debt (line of credit) sooner, thus decreasing the interest expense and netting a higher profit.

- All of this touches on cross-functional measurement. No longer is it acceptable to have business intelligence islands of information. Combining multiple measurements is the only way organizations can achieve a balanced view of their enterprise performance.

Case Study

Delivering property-casualty insurance products and services through independent brokers and agents, requires an IT infrastructure and performance-management applications that facilitate maximum collaboration. For this company, providing information to employees, to enable them to make better business decisions was critical. Plus, management identified that the right business intelligence application would encourage employees to take ownership of their data, budgets, and expenses.

> Although a large accounting system was already selected for deployment, it was apparent that the implementation process would be ongoing for years. Turning instead to a leading global business intelligence software vendor, the company had a full-blown budget system in place in two week, complete with real-time planning and a user-friendly interface that provided access over the Web. Its drill-down environment allows users to do 'what-if' scenarios and analysis on a number of levels.

Organizations need access to real-time, high quality, cross-functional data to be able to truly measure the performance of an enterprise. Once the performance is understood, there needs to be a seamless integration with actionable items, such as business plans, budgets and forecasts. It is through this unique combination that organizations will be able to break out of the constant catch-up game they have been playing with the budgets, finances and forecasts.

Up until now, even those relatively rare organizations that have used business intelligence wisely have tended to do so either with regard to performance-related issues or with regard to budgeting. The next several chapters in this book will show how both must be done if overriding end goals are to be achieved.

6

The First Piece of the Puzzle—Measure It, Manage It

Let's take a simple question: "How are we doing?" If the CEO asked this question of the CFO, the answers would most likely be in financial metrics such as "Revenue has increased twenty percent," "Cost of sales is down $45,000 this month," or "EBIT is up three percent." The same question, though, posed to the human resources VP by the COO, would most likely be in a different set of metrics, such as, "Employee attrition is up five percent this year," "Average retention time for technical staff is up to eighteen months," or "Forty percent of our managers have advanced degrees, compared to only twenty-four percent five years ago." Again, "How are we doing?" when asked to the VP of supply chain would most likely be answered in supply chain metrics, such as, "Lead time for raw materials has decreased by two days," "We have decreased our supplies from 100 to 65 over the past year," or "Average turnaround time for external products decreased by fifteen percent."

The answer to "How are we doing?" is almost always tied to function-specific metrics. Metrics, or measurable results of a business, has been an overused term by both IT and business professionals. Metrics, though, play a key role in measuring and managing the performance of an organization. Almost all business decisions are supported by some kind of metrics. Traditionally, metrics have been very focused on financial measures of an organization. Metrics such as revenue, margin, cost of goods sold, fixed overhead and such are the indicators used by the finance group and, hence, usually the most visible in an organization.

Financial measures: the tip of the iceberg

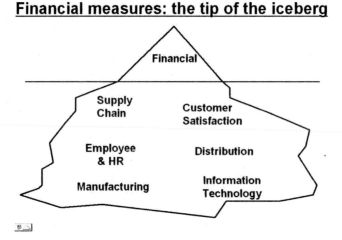

Some of these metrics may have financial components, but financial metrics need to be complemented by non-financial metrics. In most companies, financial metrics become the emergent indicators that are ultimately driven by other metrics from within the organization. The financial metrics are also most visible to investors and business partners. Additionally, the majority of figures in a traditional annual report are related to financial metrics. In actuality, financial measures only give a small glimpse into the health of an organization. Metrics from other areas such as research and development, supply chain, demand chain, human resources, and compliance, may be just as—or more—important in evaluating the organization as a whole.

Disappointingly, there are still a high number of organizations that do an adequate job at managing financial metrics, but still base many other decisions on hunches or gut feelings. This is somewhat ironic, since most organizations, from the single site manufacturer to the multi billion-dollar conglomerate, have many of the required metrics in their systems already. Through old habits, lack of knowledge of what is in their systems, or skepticism, many organizations are ignoring one of their greatest assets.

If something can be measured, whether it is in business or otherwise, it can be managed. Of course, *how* it is managed is what separates the leaders from the laggards, but many organizations do not even take the effort to measure how they are doing.

The Report Card

Imagine your child comes home from school with a report card, but there is only one subject, say math, and it is an A+. The rest of the subjects, history, physical education, writing, and science were not graded.
How could you understand and help your child with his or her performance?
This is exactly the same situation that organizations that only measure financial performance are putting themselves in every day.

The first step in using metrics is to assess the current state, or the as-is. By examining current metrics, organizations can get a report card on their situation. Adding two sets of measures from different times, such as same period last year, relative performance can be derived. If an organization does not have any real historical metrics, they can start at the present and take another snapshot in three, six or twelve months.

This ability to understand the health of an organization from a metric perspective is a major step in enhancing the management ability of the organization. It is against this baseline that changes over time can be measured. Without this baseline, managers are continually trying to hit a moving target and have little idea whether their performance is improving or declining across all functional areas.

<u>Decision Support Evolution</u>

Pre-1980
  Paper reports
1980's
  Dedicated programs & terminals
Early 1990's
  Spreadsheets, OLAP
Late 1990's
  Data Marts and Hybrid OLAP

Metric-based management dictates that decisions are supported by empirical information. Support of these decisions can be based on specific computer systems for decision support, commonly referred to as Decision Support Systems (DSS), or can be based on data from previously deployed systems for enterprise resource planning (ERP) or customer relationship management (CRM). Common to all these systems is the concept of time series. Computerized systems capture and manage information that flows across time, whether month-to-month, day-to-day, or minute-to-minute. Thus, computerized systems are best fit for providing the baseline and variance from the baseline across time.

It is this combination of metrics and time, which allows organizations to take advantage of metrics-based management, and make decisions based on metrics instead of hunches. There are still places in today's business environment for intuition and hunches. Not everything can be quantified, but efforts need to increase to provide more metrics to support the hunches and intuition of savvy business professionals. For example, an experienced sales executive may have a hunch that a new product will have a much quicker adoption time than previously released products. Why does this executive have this hunch? It could be experience, it could be memories from other products; or it could just be based on personal expectations. Very early on in the product launch, special attention should be paid to the sales metrics surrounding this product. If they are in direct support of the hunch of the executive, then the organization now has a codified model to support future product launches. If the hunch is incorrect, then the metrics can point out how the expectations of the executive differed from actual market adoption. In moving forward with metrics-proven hunches, organizations can still leverage the intuitive nature of experienced-based decisions; however, they will now be supported by concrete metrics and measurements. What's more, they can use metrics to take soft as well as hard data into account and to manage exceptions intelligently.

Metric centric decision making

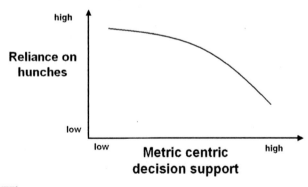

Case Study

Specializing in everything from electronics, machinery, semiconductors, and chemicals to finance, insurance and automotive, a corporate giant experienced serious compatibility issues between its worldwide ERP and the specific business analysis needs of certain geographic locations. Getting data out of the ERP system and into a format that was both familiar to users and easy to manage was paramount. On top of these requirements was the ability to graphically view data, especially for performance-driven sales and marketing teams.

The company selected a multidimensional OLAP platform that delivered power, performance, and a user-friendly Excel interface. "It provides the needed flexibility for ad-hoc reporting and the ability to calculate other information on-the-fly in Excel." This product supports the ERP, can extract data from it, and eliminates training time since users can view data in Excel.

7

What about the Soft Stuff?

A WORD ON QUANTITATIVE & QUALITATIVE DATA

In purchasing a house there are two types of information that influence the decision to buy. Quantitative information consists of hard numbers. What is the cost? Yearly taxes? Square footage? Commuting distance? Qualitative information consists of softer factors: Does the house feel roomy enough? What is the look and feel of the neighborhood? How busy are the streets?

The hard impact of soft metrics

A retail organization I worked with had a very mature financial management and reporting system. They had even implemented activity based costing. Their concentration was very financial and margin focused, but they did not have a very good handle on their non-financial, or soft metrics. Having shopped at their stores, I faced a similar frustration to other customers with wait time and scanning errors. It would have been fairly simple to monitor these metrics (turnaround time, scan error %) and find ways to improve this metric and impact corporate performance.
Instead the organization stayed heads-down on financial metrics. Later, facing financial problems, they were forced to merge with a dominant competitor.

Performance management also deals with quantitative and qualitative information. Quantitative information consists of hard numbers that can be measured. These measures include profit, revenue, number of employees, and so forth. Quantitative information can be stored in a database and shared. A previous chapter described how the measures could be used and integrated. Complementary to the quantitative information, though, is qualitative information. The following example shows different types of qualitative information, which supports the quantitative.

Let's assume that we are examining the on-time delivery performance of a company, and we have the following information:

	January	February	March	April	May	June
Number of shipments	10,300	10, 250	11,000	11,400	11,600	12,100
Percent of shipments on-time	70%	71%	70%	68%	67%	66%

A report on the above might read as follows:

Observation: Number of shipments is increasing, and on-time percentage is decreasing as the year progresses.

Opinion: Our increased shipments are causing degradation in on-time delivery percentage.

Supporting information: Delivery reports broken out by day can be attached for each month. Or, the customer may detail percentage breakout by on-time percentage.

Links: If the company uses a third party, such as UPS for delivery, a link to the UPS site explaining their service levels can be attached.

Audits: Randomly selected reports by customer can be included to support the overall number.

WHERE IS THE QUALITATIVE INFORMATION?

In most organizations, the qualitative information is spread over a number of different sources and computer systems including:

- **Files on Servers**: A common method of storing and sharing quantitative information is to put files such as documents, slides and spreadsheets on a server. The server is part of the corporate network and people from different departments can access the files and share them. The security and control processes implemented on the server can dictate limitations to the sharing.

  Sharing of files on a server has mostly replaced the older 'sneaker net' method of sharing floppy disks, but some organizations still use sneaker net for very sensitive data. Advantages of servers over sneaker nets are backup and recovery, increased ability to share files, and audit capabilities by management.

- **Email Trail**: Attaching files such as documents to email has become commonplace. A common practice is to attach a spreadsheet to an email, send the email to a colleague for modifications, and then get an email back with changes and opinions. Since most email systems allow the inclusion of a trail of the previous emails, a makeshift audit trail is created. For example a product manager prepares a cost estimate spreadsheet. She then emails the spreadsheet to her director, who examines the spreadsheet, makes comments, such as, "Please trim overhead costs by at least three percent" and sends it back to the manager. The manager then modifies her spreadsheet based on the director's comments and sends an email with the comments, "Overhead decreased by 3.4 percent" back to the director for final approval.

  For those who have been through this cycle, we know that it almost never ends with one email exchange. The trail tends to get larger and larger. Another problem is that if someone starts a new email exchange without the history, or segues to a new subject, the email trail is in effect broken. Someone wanting a complete history will need to figure out which emails were sent and their chronological order. The whole process very quickly becomes messy and error-prone as well as time-consuming.

- **Intranet**: An intranet is an internal company Internet site for sharing information. Sometimes it is accessed via a company portal. Intranets are usually deployed by larger organizations, but the decreasing cost of implementing the technology has allowed mid-size companies to build intranets as well. An intranet is usually built by a centralized information technology group and can contain everything from the company's human resource manual to discussion groups to file sharing areas. Intranets usually require significant information technology resources, including staff, hardware and software, to keep them up to date. This large cost often raises doubts in an organization as to whether the benefits justify the investment. Too often, the IT department builds and maintains the intranet based on their technical desires, and loses touch with the required business benefit. So, while the IT department is implementing the latest Java applet, or graphics, the business community still cannot get their basic information.

Successful intranets are driven by business needs and benefits. The intranet will require technical resources including staff, hardware and software, but in a successful intranet each expenditure of IT resources is cost justified.

- **Paper**: The age of the paperless office has produced more paper than ever. Many senior managers still rely heavily on printed reports, memos, and briefs. There are some executives who still will not use email. This legacy of paper dependence does not show any sign of diminishing, but the shortcomings of paper are myriad. They include: lost papers, duplicate information, and loss of critical information when an employee leaves.

SHARING DIFFERENT KINDS OF QUALITATIVE INFORMATION IN DIFFERENT WAYS

Different types of qualitative information are shared in different ways. Preferences tend to depend on the type of information being shared and, sometimes, to technical considerations. Although any method could be used for each type of qualitative information, there are at least four primary methods used for sharing different types of qualitative information.

	Observation	Opinion	Supporting	Links	Audits
Servers					
Email Trail	Primary	Primary	Primary		Primary
Intranet				Primary	
Paper					

As we can see, we have created a business environment with an increased dependence on email. We are in the process of attaching more and more information to a format that was not designed for being a sharing and collaboration database. Although newer offerings from Microsoft and IBM are combining the collaboration and emailing capabilities, their true benefits have yet to be realized.

OPTIMIZING QUALITATIVE AND QUANTITATIVE INFORMATION
Combining Qualitative and Quantitative

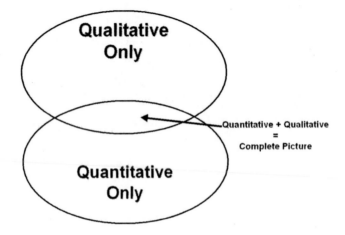

The optimal solution is to have the qualitative and quantitative information stored with and connected to each other. For example, if the sales figures for February are $405,000 for North America, and this is twenty percent above the projected amount, the ability to view a reasoning or explanation from the North American Sales Manager concurrently with examining the actual sales figures would be the best solution. In many organizations, this simple process of connecting qualitative and quantitative information together, in real-time, is limited by the existing computer programs and networks.

When evaluating technical solutions to performance management, the combination of qualitative and quantitative information must be given high importance. There is still more to the story, however. Once concrete metrics and measurements are in place, the organization can begin to perform the critical function of benchmarking itself. That is the subject of the next chapter.

Case Study

A pioneer in the computer networking industry for more than two decades, a vendor was trying to collect forecast data and then track it by region and by customer. At the time, the division had 120 customers worldwide and was dealing with approximately 2,000 SKUs. Despite the enormity of the task, the forecasts were being tracked in an Excel spreadsheet. It was a cumbersome, serial process that the company was eager to change.

A database driven solution that would allow multiple concurrent users, including those in remote locations, was identified as the best solution. By changing from Excel to a system that offered forecasting functionality, evaluating how a given product line was doing against forecast became a breeze. The capacity to analyze and collaborate–leading to sound business decisions–has resulted from moving to the right performance management tools.

8

Benchmarks—Your Performance Tailor

Buying a new business outfit can sometimes be a challenge. Besides determining the proper color, style and fabric, there is the stressful situation of trying on the clothes and seeing if you still are that dress size 8 or suit size 42. It is very rare that an adult's clothing size remains the same and never requires tailoring, such as shortening the hem or taking in the waist.

There is a distinct method to sizing a suit. First you determine you're off the shelf size. Next, you determine your variation (42 Short, 44 Long, etc.). Then the tailor determines your modifications (shorten sleeves, let out waist, cuff the pants, etc.). The tailor does this by taking measurements of your arms, legs, torso, and neck, making recommendations for modifications to make the suit fit.

With business benchmarking, the method is nearly identical. First, determine your industry (insurance, manufacturing, food & hospitality, etc.). Next determine your variation within that industry. Are you a large, mid or small market player? Third, tailor the benchmark to your individual needs. Do you have a dominant product line? What is your customer mix? Are you growing or stabilized?

Underperforming and Overperforming

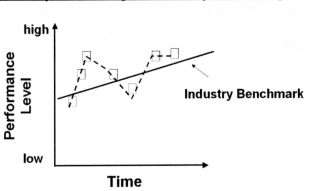

In the end you will have a benchmark fit to your particular needs. Just like most people will not fit an off the shelf suit, most organizations do not fit into off the shelf benchmarks.

BENCHMARKS AND THEIR ROLE IN PERFORMANCE MANAGEMENT

In purchasing a home, one of the key factors is a market survey. The market survey shows what local homes have been listed and selling for over the past year. Based on similar homes and the condition of the prospective homes, prices are set and negotiated. If an average 2,200-square foot home with three bedrooms and 2 ½ baths is selling for $250,000 in a neighborhood, a homeowner with a similar house should list somewhere in the general area of $250,000. Listing prices are not usually arbitrary and are based on some benchmarks of previous relevant sales.

In measuring the performance of a business, benchmarks play a very similar role. Measuring a business' profitability or customer satisfaction is useful. Adding relativity to these numbers, though are benchmarks, or industry acceptable values. Many organizations attempt to, and sometimes succeed at measuring their results, but very few compare these measurements to acceptable levels of their industry peers. Obtaining a true indication of the health of an organization requires the planned, actual and benchmark values for a complete view.

BENCHMARKS—WHERE TO GET THEM

Benchmarks are often available from industry groups, government, management consultants, academic sources, and the Internet. Which benchmark is the right one for your organization? Maybe the better question is which benchmarks are not right for your organization. We have all heard the quip that "studies show that eighty percent of all statistics are made up." With the proliferation of the Internet, email, and other electronic communications, the risk of false or misleading benchmarks has greatly increased. Anyone with an official-sounding URL, like **www.benchmark-institute.com** and some simple web programming can pass themselves off as a legitimate benchmarking organization.

This is not to say that all benchmarks obtained from Internet sites are bogus. However, regardless of the source, whether it is from a book, consultant or Internet site, validity needs to be verified.

Academic vs. Pragmatic Benchmarks

Many academic organizations produce performance benchmarks. Some of these benchmarks are extremely academic in their use and applicability. The measures being used may not be practical in real-world scenarios. Some people may remember the movie *Back to School* with Rodney Dangerfield from the 1980s. In a business class, the professor describes the requirements for starting a new business producing widgets. Dangerfield's character then starts to contradict the professor, citing his experience from dealing with builders, unions, etc. Although the situation is fictional, some correlation can be drawn from an academic view of benchmarks versus commercial view of benchmarks. Businesses require pragmatic, usable benchmarks to measure their performance. Do not dismiss the academic benchmarks, but do question their pragmatic application.

Challenges of Sharing Data

Benchmarks, because they touch on the key performance indicators of an organization, delve into the area of protected data. Many publicly traded organizations are reluctant to share information beyond what is available in the financial disclosures and annual reports. Privately held organizations keep their cards even closer to their vest, since they are required to disclose little if any information, except to the IRS.

Professional organizations responsible for collecting benchmarks must ensure that they protect the data of the respondents. As more companies contribute to the benchmarks, the statistical confidence rating increases, which makes the benchmarks more valuable. Thus, finding a common ground where organizations will share their performance measurements, while still feeling safe, is key.

Internal Benchmarking

In absence of access to external benchmarks, many organizations will use internal benchmarks. These benchmarks represent an internal view of historical performance and may have been created from a number of sources.

Merger Data

A most common source of internal benchmarks is those arising from pre-and post-analysis of mergers.

In preparation for mergers, organizations attempt to find the best scenario for achieving optimal performance from the newly merged organization. Historical views of the separate companies will yield trends and performance indicators. During the preparation for the merger or valuation phase, this understanding of past performance becomes critical.

This benchmark collection process can be used in the post-merger situation.

<u>Consulting Engagements</u>

Many management-consulting firms will sell engagements to benchmark an organization. In many cases, these benchmarks are underutilized and end up in some manager's file cabinet. Since the consulting firm probably charged a hefty sum of money and took up a fair amount of management's time to create these benchmarks, they should be utilized whenever possible. The risks involved with using the results of consulting engagement benchmarks are related to timeliness and applicability. Benchmarks can become stale. In organizations that have a high velocity of change (see Velocity of Change chapter), consultant-created benchmarks may have a shelf life of six months or less. It is critical for management to understand the timeliness of the benchmarks created during previous consulting engagements. Benchmarks may also not be applicable. The reality of many of the benchmarks created during consulting engagements is that they are ultimately used by the consulting firm as a sales device to sell more billable hours. Thus, the benchmarks may do a good job at pointing out the weak performance points, but may not highlight the strong points. Balanced benchmarks must adequately represent the good with the bad.

ATTRIBUTES OF A QUALITY BENCHMARK

There are five attributes of a quality benchmark: relevance, accessibility, timeliness, component-based and multidimensionality. Each of these attributes will determine the usability and value of a benchmark to an organization.

Benchmark Quality Attribute 1—Relevance

Benchmarks need to have relevance to the organization using them. The benchmarks need to be from the same or similar industry. For example, a food and hospitality industry benchmark may have little relevance to a financial services industry. Since many industries become specialized, a benchmark for a specific business model may not be available, but the benchmarks should be as relevant to their industry as possible.

The relevance is also affected by the geography. If an organization is focused on a tri-state area, benchmarks for multi-national conglomerates may not be appropriate. Also, some industries, such as health-care, vary greatly from geographic region to region. Similar to the industry, the geography should be as specific as is possible.

Relevance is also affected by size. Size can be measured financially, such as annual revenue, or by number of employees. Size of companies represented in the benchmark should be as close as possible to the organization. Many benchmarks offer values for different sizes of organizations, such as less than $50M, $51M—$500M, and $500M+. In this case, organizations should choose the size that most closely represents their own.

Benchmark Quality Attribute 2—Accessibility

Similar to any other data used for decision support, accessibility will impact the quality of the benchmark. Of particular importance are: one time versus repeated use, proprietary format and technology, and connectivity to external systems.

One time vs. Repeated Use

In searching for benchmarks, organizations will be able to find a one-time use scenario. If the organization needed to take a single view of their performance against the benchmark, this would be the most likely use. More realistic, though, is that organizations will require repeated access to the benchmarks. This brings an organization to the point where they must decide to purchase or license the data or pay a consulting firm to create the benchmarks. The purchase/license option allows for frequent and repeated use of the data and more freedom from dependence on a consulting firm. Organizations will also need to weigh the cost of licensing versus paying the consultants, along with the cost of retaining employees who understand and can use the benchmarks

Proprietary Format and Technology

If an organization is planning on licensing or purchasing the benchmarks, special attention needs to be given to the technology in which the benchmarks will be presented. Proprietary formats and technology refers to the physical means, which the benchmarks are stored in a computer system or database. Since many benchmarking organization are also interested in selling consulting services to accompany the benchmarks, they will keep the data in a proprietary format. Proprietary data results in the organization's inability to use their existing information technology staff to read and manipulate the data. Worse than a proprietary format, though, is proprietary technology. Some organizations will use cryptic databases that can only be used and unlocked by the benchmark provider. Thus, even if an organization could understand the format of the data being provided, they would still have limited access because of not being able to communicate with the underlying database.

It is always desirable to have the benchmarks provided in a standard format and standard technology. In a standard format, the names of fields would adequately represent the content of the data. For example, a field named *revenue* would represent the revenue of the company. Standard technology, such as Microsoft or Oracle databases, are always more desirable to cryptic flat file systems as well.

Connectivity to External Systems

Some benchmarks are only provided by subscribing to a system, which is not controlled by the licensing company. Each time a benchmark needs to be compared or queried, a user must sign on to a system at the benchmarking company. This is an undesirable situation from a usability perspective, because the user can never fully integrate the benchmarks with the actual values of the organization. External systems, though, have an advantage in that the organization needs to provide little or no technical maintenance. The maintenance of the data and the system are outsourced to the benchmark provider.

Organizations need to compare the cost and benefits of external systems vs. bringing the data in-house. If an organization retains a sufficient information technology staff, bringing the benchmarks in-house is most likely the best choice.

Benchmark Quality Attribute 3—Timeliness

Benchmarks need to be assessed for timeliness. There are two aspects of timeliness that need to be considered: history period and currency. A combination of these two attributes will help determine the quality of the benchmark.

History Period

Benchmarks are historical views of performance. The historical period can be long or short term. A problem with this is that what is long term to one industry, may be short term to another. For example, a benchmark that measures three years of performance may be adequate for an emerging business, such as online content provider. But for an established business with a slower velocity of change, such as the steel industry company, three years may not be an adequate historical period.

The historical period needs to take into account any known seasonality issues or cyclical behavior. The benchmark needs to include multiple seasonal or cyclical iterations. For example, the performance of financial services companies will follow the cyclical nature of the stock market, in general. These cycles may take three months or four years to complete. A true benchmark would have enough data to cover at least two up periods and two down periods, allowing statistical confidence to be high.

<u>Currency</u>

Currency is also key for the historical view of performance. A benchmark must be from a relevant point in time and avoid the staleness of older data. This is especially true in volatile economic times, where business models change rapidly.

Benchmark Quality Attribute 4—Component Based

Benchmarks are comprised of various components such as financial measures, productivity measures, market share, and supply-chain data. Although a complete view of these cross-functional measures will usually provide the highest business value, it is not always the best view. Component-based benchmarks allow organizations to pick and choose the benchmarks they will use and only license those benchmarks. Similar to the automobile with the luxury package, which contains leather, tilt steering, heated mirrors, etc., there are economies of scale in purchases the whole benchmark package. With the automobile, every driver requires not every part of the luxury package. In benchmarking, an organization may only want to concentrate on market share benchmarks and will defer other benchmarks until a later date. Why then should the organization be burdened with purchasing the whole package up front?

This, once again, is a business decision, based on cost-benefit analysis.

Benchmark Quality Attribute 5—Multidimensional Benchmarks

Multidimensionality refers to the ability to view the benchmarks within different contexts and hierarchies. Typical dimensions include geography (city, state, country), product (SKU, brand, division) and time (month, quarter, year). The most desirable situation is that the benchmarks are multidimensional and have the ability to be examined and analyzed in one or more dimensional contexts (for example, examining the benchmark of food products in Washington state, or February average collection by brand).

Benchmark Quality Attributes
1. Relevance
2. Accessibility
3. Timeliness
4. Component-based
5. Multidimensional

Since, though, benchmarks are generally collected from companies that do not carry the exact same products or manage geographies similarly, the data may not be available at this level. Benchmarks are generally provided at the lowest common denominator with regards to multidimensionality. Organizations must extrapolate the benchmarks to their level of detail or use the aggregated level provided by the benchmark.

BENCHMARK BREAKPOINTS

When a teenager receives his or her driver's license, there is usually a major shift in their activities as well as level of responsibility. They become more mobile and independent, but also must support this change with responsibilities such as insurance payments and maintenance of their car. Businesses often reach certain breakpoints where their operations or business plans will change. This can be impacted by external events such as market conditions or increased competition, or internal events, such as management changes or equity structure modifications.

Special attention needs to given to the breakpoint of a business and how benchmarks can be impacted by these breakpoints. The first place to look for these breakpoints is the past. Has the company gone public recently? Have new product lines been introduced or old ones retired? Has there been a merger? Has the company opened a new sales channel? These are examples of changes that could constitute a breakpoint.

Breakpoints impact performance

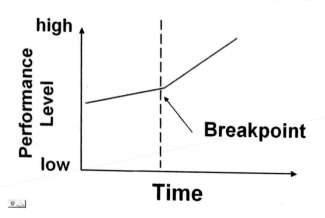

Some benchmarks will remain relevant throughout an organization. Examples of constant benchmarks are revenue per employee, product R&D costs, and net income. Regardless of whether or not there has been a breakpoint, these measures will still mean something to decision makers.

Some measures may only become relevant after a breakpoint. If a company has recently gone public, price to earnings (P/E) ratio becomes a new relevant measure. If a company has made a change from single nation to multinational focus, ratio of sales from national versus international sources becomes relevant.

Organizations need to understand and classify benchmarks as they apply to constants or breakpoints. Each time a business model changes, the organization should re-examine the relevancy of their current benchmarks and look for other more relevant measures.

CONSTANT VS. PERIODIC REVIEW

Earlier, we discussed the subject of one-time versus recurring benchmarks. A related issue is how the benchmarks will be administered in monitoring performance. There are three types of review: periodic, constant and hybrid.

Periodic Benchmarking

Periodic reviews select a fixed time frame in which the performance will be measured against the benchmarks. Take the example of the tailoring of a suit. You must first know your size when you are preparing to purchase your new suit. Generally, periodic reviews can range from quarterly to every three years or more. With periodic reviews, the organization measures past performance against a benchmark. They will then gather their actual values over a set period of time, for example, a quarter. After the quarter is over, they will then repeat the historical measurement of their performance using an extrapolation of the benchmark.

Periodic benchmarks will also need to be adjusted after breakpoints to establish a new performance expectation. If a breakpoint is encountered or expected, a new benchmark and extrapolation should be created.

Periodic benchmarking requires a five-step methodology:

1. Create or acquire the applicable benchmark. Using the criteria listed above, an organization should pick the appropriate benchmark for their application.

2. Determine the as-is and compare to the benchmark. The current performance of the organization should be compared to the benchmark with special attention paid to large variances.

3. Plot the to-be benchmark at a desired future time. This can be quarterly, yearly, etc. The to-be can use the benchmark to extrapolate out to what would be the expected benchmark performance.

4. Use internal tracking to gather required data. Once the data is gathered, it can be used at the end of the prescribed time frame to determine actual vs. benchmark. This will also be valuable input in to step 5.

5. Select the new benchmark for the next period. This will be determined by applying the analysis in step 4 along with applicable updates to the benchmark. This five-step process is then repeated for the new benchmark.

Constant Benchmarking

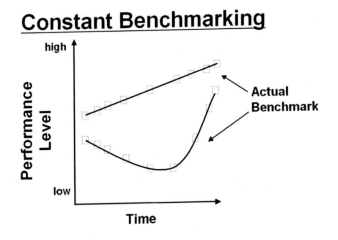

Constant benchmarking involves a consistent checking of performance against an acquired benchmark. This is similar trying on your suit every day even if you are not going to wear the suit. For some industries—particularly, industries that have quick business lifecycles from product inception to retirement of the company, constant benchmarking is the correct approach. This could be said of the late 1990s dot-com companies. Many of these organizations were working on a short lifecycle and the companies were targeting exit strategies in twelve-month timeframes. With this in mind, an annual benchmark did not make sense.

Constant benchmarking, though, requires a significant commitment of time and resources to the benchmark and monitoring process. This was not possible for the dot-coms of yesteryear. Thus, constant benchmarking offers a paradox of the companies that can most likely benefit do not have the ability or resource to take advantage of the benchmarks.

Hybrid Benchmarking

Hybrid benchmarking combines attributes of constant and periodic benchmarking. This is like knowing you are a size 42, but that consistently your sleeves need alterations. First, a benchmark is taken for the as-is. Second, a to-be is plotted for a short periodic time in the future, usually twelve months or less. The company collects the required data during the time period to be able to measure performance against the to-be benchmark. A new to-be for moving into the future is then determined based on the results of the actual performance, variance from the expected to-be, and a new forward-looking benchmark.

The greatest benefit of hybrid benchmarking is that organizations can use their own measured performance to fine-tune the next-to-be benchmark. This allows the objectivity of the external benchmark and the strength of using actual values from your organization as a differentiator.

In this way, the hybrid benchmark combines both the added benefit of constant benchmarking and the statistical averaging of the periodic benchmark. Most important is that the hybrid benchmark process involves nearly the same amount of effort as the periodic method, but has the potential to deliver much higher returns. Organizations examining periodic benchmark should examine hybrids as a cost-effective alternative.

LACK OF BENCHMARKS

Many people believe benchmarks belong exclusively in the realm of large, global 1000 organizations. The mid-market company may think that the benchmarks are out their reach for either cost or accessibility reasons. There are a number of ways in which mid-market companies can take advantage of the power of benchmarking, though.

Consultants

Many accounting and consulting firms that target the mid-market have cost effective solutions for benchmarking. This has also created a downward pressure on the large consulting firms to provide offerings to the mid-market.

Internal History

"There's no place like home" can be applied to benchmarking. Many organizations have been collecting financial, customer, product development, supply chain and organizational data for years. Through proper organization of this data, a company may have an inexpensive access to their own benchmarks. Existing technologies such as data warehouses and business intelligence systems, make this process of collecting the data repeatable and less technology dependent. Organizations can normally collect this data and organize it using existing information technology staff and resources with small investments in some new technology tools.

Previous Experience & Know How

Internal history refers to data in the computer systems of an organization. There is also a wealth of benchmarking knowledge that is not stored in the computer systems, though. Information technology people refer to this as unstructured data. Some organizations implement knowledge management systems (complex technology to store and share this unstructured data). This, though, is typically a long and expensive process that may or may not offer a measurable return on investment (ROI).

A growing trend is to allow parts of this unstructured data to be tied directly to either benchmark or actual performance data. (See Chapter—Integrating Qualitative Information) For example, an agricultural product company may be tracking sales volume versus projected sales volume. In one month, there is a large dip in actual sales, and the sales manager can explain this through extreme weather in the previous weeks. Many computer systems can allow a short memo or note to be tied directly to the sales figure.

The benefit of tying directly to the value is that in measuring the performance against the benchmark, the explanation is attached to the values instead of having to be discovered through an email trail or meeting notes.

Case Study:

A major tire manufacturer needed speed and reliability when it came to performance-management data. Its previous system, which involved a spreadsheet-based management information system, was becoming far too complex and difficult to maintain. Although management wanted to report information in a number of different dimensions, numerous spreadsheets were not what they had in mind.

By partnering with a leading software vendor, the company has made the shift from spreadsheets to optimal productivity. Users report a smooth transition and reports are produced instantly from one data source. Changing or restating information is never a problem, and pinpointing variances to see where problems exist takes moments instead of months.

TODAY'S VALUES—TOMORROW'S BENCHMARKS

If organizations use their existing computer systems to capture the actual values now, these can be the benchmarks of tomorrow. Important, though, is not only capturing the actual values, but all of the adjusted forecasts and plans. This will allow organizations to create perspective versus actual views and guide their future benchmarking efforts.

Now we have looked at using benchmarks to compare youself to others in the industry and discover how you can improve your position. But things never remain static; rather they are in constant flux. To make the benchmarks more relevant, the next step is to compare and contrast various 'what if' scenarios. Our next chapter, therefore, addresses the topic of predictive modeling.

9

Predictive Modeling—the Power of What-If

One of the most challenging tasks for parents is planning for and funding a college education for their children. What was considered normal college costs even ten years ago cannot even be considered a low estimate today. Assuming that parents have some foresight and start saving at an early age, they need to make some key assumptions based on future scenarios. What if college costs double every seven years? What if levels of available financial aid do not change as the mean family income does? What if we pick a private college as opposed to a public one? What if we choose commuting instead of on campus housing? Answers to each of these what if questions will likely yield a different savings strategy.

Surprising enough, most organizations do not factor even this relatively rudimentary level of "what if" into their budgeting and planning process. Imagine trying to save for college costs based on assumptions that today's cost of living and college costs will not change.

THE CURRENT STATE OF BUDGETING AND PLANNING

Many organizations have a strategic plan in the form of mission statements and goals. Usually quite lofty, such as 'relentless pursuit of customer satisfaction' or 'market leadership,' these strategic plans many times do not reach the level of tactical implementation. When it comes time for the tactical plan, most organizations still rely on the annual budgeting and planning cycle. This process, which in some larger organizations can take up to six months, is usually based on a twelve-month time horizon. Organizations will start budgeting and planning for the following year in the third or fourth quarter and will use this budget to guide their expenditures and expectations throughout the next year.

This process, even in medium-sized organizations, is typically one of the most bureaucratic activities of the year. Often times, whole departments will be dedicated to the budget and nothing but the budget for months. Forward-reaching projects are put on hold to complete budgets. Endless meetings are scheduled. Emails are circulated to large distribution groups. During this process, many cost center managers are very concerned with protecting his or her individual budgets. So, although there is considerable time expended on this budgeting and planning process, much of it is not productive toward the end result.

The centralized finance organization, which is ultimately responsible for delivering the budget to the CFO, is faced with challenges of their own. With the trend toward globalization, there are increased challenges with geographies. The managers who will provide the data may be spread throughout the globe. This also introduces the challenge of time zone differences. Anyone who has done business where international collaboration and communication are required in real-time, fully understands the challenge of having very early morning or very late evening meetings and conference calls.

Many organizations also face increased technical challenges. Most budgeting systems are built on spreadsheet technology and have grown more complex as the years have passed. What started out as a simple spreadsheet may have turned into a set of fifty sheets with intra-and inter—sheet links. Often, the origin of the sheets and the associated formulas are not be known. Organizations will stay with this process as creatures of habit. Another technical challenge may be faced by organizations that have various technical platforms. Many times, one division of a company will be using a particular platform for their financial systems, while another division may be using a second platform that is incompatible.

The 3 P's challenging budgeting and planning

Process
often disjoint or undocumented
People
lack of time and attention
Power
technical ability of existing systems

In this current budgeting and planning process, there is also a significant amount of effort spent on correcting quality problems in the data. For example, a cost center may have used one formula to determine gross profit, while the corporate organization used another. The central finance organization is now forced to change the data many times. Re-entry is susceptible to errors, like any data entry process. Improperly entered data may not even be detected until all the spreadsheets are consolidated. By then, it may be too late to regather the original figures from the cost centers, and a best guess may be needed.

Due to this bureaucratic process and the vast amount of manual data entry and rework, many organizations have little or no time to concentrate on anything more than a twelve-month planning horizon. Focusing beyond the next year would require even more data entry and consolidation, and the organization would risk not having the budget completed by the beginning of the upcoming year. The main focus is on getting the figures and making sure they balance.

MOVING TO THE WHAT-IF

Similar to the college planning exercise, organizations need to take advantage of the power of what-if. If the budgeting cycle can be streamlined, more time can be spent on performing what-if analysis. This enables organizations to model possible outcomes based on major or even minor changes and understand their ultimate possible impact on the business. Organizations are able to understand the impact of major moves, such as adding or closing a plant to minor adjustments like changing the list price on one product. Although the latter may seem quite minor in the large scheme, ultimate impacts could be extensive.

When evaluating what-if scenarios, changes are magnified by time and quantity. The college comparison is quite relevant in this case. If the parents are planning on an average annual return of five percent and have planned this for the next ten years, but the return averages to three percent, the end result could be the difference between Ivy League and State U.

When examining major changes in organizations, impacts may actually be easier to understand, since there is usually some known cause-and-effect pattern. Closing plants will usually result in cost savings. Introducing new products will usually create revenue, but it will also incur new marketing or research costs.

Understanding the minor changes and their ultimate impact proves more difficult. Assume that a company has 1,000 distinct products or SKUs and they are sold through twenty-five different sales offices. Next, assume the product manager from one of the SKUs decides to decrease the list price by one percent along with making a host of other pricing changes. What the product manager may not know is that particular SKU is responsible for 60% of the sales for the two most profitable sales offices. So, instead of a minor product pricing change, major impacts will be seen in the bottom line. The impact of this change may not be seen until it is too late and the profits from the two sales offices have dwindled. It is this combination of the time and quantity, which have turned the minor change into a major business impact.

THE SCENARIO BASED PLANNING ENVIRONMENT

To address the problem of minor adjustments becoming major business impacts through time and quantity, organizations must embrace a scenario-based planning environment (SBPE). In the SBPE, impacts of minor changes are seen before actual capital or resources are expended. SBPE dictates that modeling and understanding the impact can be done without having to commit business resources and money. In a model-based environment, iterations of changes can be tested and their impact can be seen immediately. Organizations can avoid costly entrances into new business models that may ultimately fail.

Freeing time from Static Budgeting

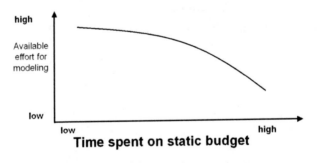

Organizations spending high amounts of time on static budgets have little availability for modeling

In a SBPE, more effort is spent in modeling and understanding the impact. Instead of using the majority of effort in creating a single budget through gathered information, many budget scenarios are created and analyzed. There are four enablers of SBPE: change-adaptable environment, metrics-based decision-making, collaboration, and technology.

First and foremost is that an organization must be *change adaptable*. If upper management will not accept any change to their process, any changes will fail. Upper management must be open to changing such core processes as budgeting and planning. Many times this is not an issue. Pose the question "What do you think of your budgeting process?" To many organizations and the answers will range from a rolling of eyes to adequate. It is very rare for an organization to brag that they have the best budget process. Management recognizes that there is usually room for improvement.

Organizations that use *metrics based decision-making* embrace measurements, historical data, and metrics for supporting decisions. This is the second enabler of SBPE. These organizations have evolved beyond making business decisions based on hunches. They also realize that if there are metrics and measurements for past decisions, the organization can use this information to support better, more informed decisions. Metrics-based decision-making many times does not require sophisticated and overburdened information systems. In many cases, information can be delivered through familiar interfaces, such as spreadsheets.

Metrics must reach well beyond the traditional top-line measurements, such as aggregated gross revenue or earnings per share. The metrics required for supporting decisions must be available at mid and high levels of detail. For example, profit contribution can be measured at a product line or cost-center level.

The third enabler of SBPE is *collaboration*. Collaboration is a term often misused by technologists. *Webster Collegiate Dictionary* defines collaboration as—to work jointly with others or together especially in an intellectual endeavor. Although technology can be an enabler of collaboration, technology should not be a driver of collaboration. The SBPE organization will understand and leverage the process of collaboration and pick the appropriate technologies to support the process. If the organization needs to perform scenario-based planning across disparate geographic regions, they may opt for a more Web-based collaborative environment. If, though, all people are located centrally, the introduction of Web-based collaboration may be overkill. Instead, the organization could implement a centralized shared budget application and use their local area network (LAN) to enable the collaboration.

Collaboration enables organizations to take advantage of a SBPE in real-time. As product managers are forecasting at brand or product levels, the cost center managers are evaluating and adjusting the impact on the bottom line. Without collaboration, there would be delays in understanding impact and there would also be increased manual coordination between different departments.

The fourth enabler is *technology*. As described above, different drivers, such as geography and organizational design, will help an organization select the type of technology to be used. The most important factor in technology is the ability to support both centralized and decentralized processes within one environment. If the technology requires managers to enter data in one system for products and another for costs, the manual process will lead to lost productivity and increased errors.

The technical platform should also be based on existing or emerging standards. This will guard against proprietary obsolescence. By investing in standards-based technologies, an organization will extend the longevity of the systems and increase the overall return on investment.

The technical platform should also provide built-in functionality, which is common to modeling and planning scenarios. Functions that relate to financial modeling, allocation, time-series analysis, and exception reporting should be included, since these are common functions regardless of industry or sector. Organizations may use the built-in functionality in unique combinations and iterations, but the basic functions that form the building blocks remain common.

BECOMING AN **SBPE** ORGANIZATION

There is a three-phase methodology that an organization must follow to become an SBPE organization. The trio of phases: model the as-is process, model the to-be, and implement the technical environment; these must be performed in sequence.

Model the As-is

The current state of business process must be understood and analyzed. This will provide a starting point. More importantly, understanding the existing state points out the shortcomings in the current process.

An organization must be able to understand and model how they currently perform planning. Most likely, this will involve multiple departments and groups. In modeling the as-is, an organization will need to understand the data that is used, how that data is shared, when decision points are reach, and what the conflict resolution strategy is.

1. Data Selection

    Selecting the data to use is the cornerstone of this process. The granularity, or level of the data is important. The further the level of detail, the greater the possibility for performing more detailed planning. Besides granularity, the functional applicability of the data is also important. With functional applicability, data is examined for the number of business functions represented. These include marketing, research, and sales. In many organizations, each function has its own data points that can hinder the creation of true business scenarios. Organizations must pay particular attention to the adaptability of the data points to other parts of the organization.

    This sharing of the data across functions is a result of both organizational design and technical considerations. Many organizations have unknowingly built up islands of responsibility within them, with little or no view toward a holistic view of the data. In addition, many older technologies prescribe to proprietary formats and storage mechanisms. So, even if the organization were redesigned to promote sharing, there might still be a technical undertaking.

2. Decision Points

    As this data flows throughout an organization, the *decision points* need to be modeled. Ultimately, the planning process is a chain of decision points with expanding realm of control for each decision. The current process may have departmental managers preparing plans and then passing them on to divisional management. Once divisional management has agreed and passed the plan on to the central finance organization, the control of the decision is out of the hands of the departmental manager. Understanding and modeling this decision tree is key to understanding the as-is process.

3. Conflict Resolution

    Just as important, though, is the *conflict resolution* strategy. As the centralized organization is consolidating plans from each division, there will be adjustments. Funds may have to be moved from R&D to sales, or from one product line to another. This may ultimately create an internal conflict. It is key for an organization to understand and document the conflict resolution strategy for planning.

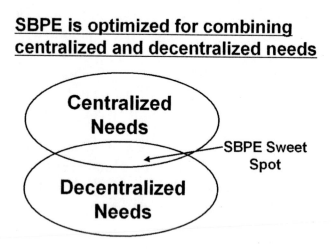

SBPE is optimized for combining centralized and decentralized needs

Model the To-be Process

Not every organization will find it beneficial to use the same desired SBPE process. There are a number of factors that will impact their choice of to-be, including: velocity of change within the industry, technical adaptability, and management's span of control.

Velocity of Change

Velocity of change is defined as the speed at which business models must adjust to changing business environments. Depending on the specific industry, velocity of change can be quite different. Generally, the more an industry is dependent on newer technology, the higher the velocity of change. For example, the biotech industry revolves around the introduction of new technologies. Their velocity of change is high. Changes happen very often and very quickly. The real estate industry uses technology, but is generally not very dependent on newer technologies to remain viable. Thus, the velocity of change is low. Changes do not happen very often and not very quickly.

In modeling the to-be SBPE process, understanding the impact of velocity of change will impact the overall process. In high velocity of change environments, organizations must design a SBPE process that enables on-the-fly modeling with an emphasis on quick turnaround of scenarios. The SBPE process must enable rapid modeling of what-if upon what-if scenarios. This may mean that less detailed data is used in the interest of timeliness in the creating of scenarios. It also may mean a more centralized control of the planning process, in the interest of speeding up the on-the-fly modeling capabilities.

Lower velocity of change industries, will have the ability to create more thorough and detailed what-if models. Also, because the technology is changing at a slower pace for this industry, a fewer number of what-if scenarios may be required.

Understanding and using the velocity of change is key in modeling the to-be process.

Technical Adaptability

Technical adaptability applies to the organization's ability to absorb and assimilate to new technologies in the planning process. If the organization is using the same circa-1990 mainframe programs for planning and have not embraced newer technologies without great resistance, they will have a lower technical adaptability. Organizations, though, which have implemented newer technologies, such as databases and intranets, without negative business or productivity impact, have a much higher technical adaptability. Technical adaptability must be understood and built in the new SBPE process.

Management Span of Control

The to-be SBPE process must fit within management's span of control. If a single division of a company plans to implement a SBPE process, it is not realistic to expect other division to also automatically adopt SBPE. Management must recognize this in building the to-be SBPE process. The process can take into account, but should not expect to change processes outside management's span of control. This is also true for business partners and vendors. If an organization is dependent on data from business partners to create business scenarios, they may request this data from their partners. There should, though, be realistic expectations of what requests will be honored. Many times, business partners do not have the level of detail or timeliness of data required for the optimal SBPE process.

Each of these factors: velocity of change, technical adaptability, and management's span of control will contribute to the design of the to-be SBPE process.

Implement the Technical Environment

With an understanding of the as-is process and the modeled to-be process, the proper technology must be implemented to support the transition to the new process. This technology must be able to support the data's level of detail, turnaround time for scenarios, and online collaboration.

Different systems allow varying levels of detail in the data that can be captured and managed. One of the shortcomings of many traditional budgeting computer systems is that they cannot support both the low level detail (such as SKU, project or cost level) and highly aggregated data (such as division or legal entity) in the same computer application. Key technology platform selection criteria for organizations moving to SBPE must be the ability of to support detailed and aggregated data in the same application.

With this level of detail, the computer system must also have the ability to provide acceptable turnaround time for scenarios. In a rapidly moving environment, it is often unacceptable to wait for overnight processing. Many times, on-the-fly, real-time scenario generation and evaluation are required. This can often be difficult for many monolithic systems that were not designed for quick turnaround.

The fast turnaround of detailed and aggregated data should not sacrifice the advantages of online collaboration. Although spreadsheets can provide much of the detailed data in a timely fashion, collaboration is limited to sharing or emailing files. An optimal technical environment would combine the speed and ease of use of spreadsheets with an industrial-strength database, making sharing and collaboration possible.

Three technical building blocks of SBPE

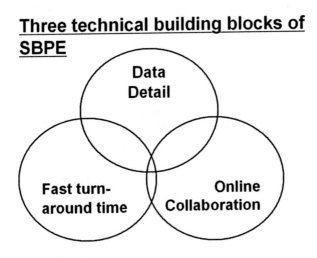

These three criteria, data detail, quick turnaround time, and online collaboration are the building blocks for selecting an implementing the technical environment to support the SBPE.

SBPE offers significant advantages to organizations when performing, planning, and budgeting. By moving from the 'what happened' to the 'what-if' mindset, organizations can take advantage of their existing planning process, while better preparing for changes in the future. They can also take advantage of the velocity of change. SBPE requires an upfront understanding of the current process, the to-be process and the technology to enable the new environment. Following a process-centric approach in order to drive the new technical environment will allow organizations to build new planning process, which in turn will give them a greater competitive advantage.

Case Study:

One of the world's leading providers of imaging and information products, including film, cameras, color print systems, and data tapes and cartridges, had an inflexible mainframe housing its financials, budgets, and expense controls. It was not unusual for this company's controller to spend extraordinary amounts of time downloading data from the mainframe, feeding the data into an Access database, then running the end result in an Excel spreadsheet. The process was time-consuming and far from state-of-the-art, and the controller knew he needed a more efficient solution.

A powerful integrated software product was implemented, able to rapidly perform multiple and complex consolidations and handle the most elaborate business models and calculations. These new capabilities made the analysis of the impact of a change in a business rule or consolidation path immediate, versus what took hours to construct previously. The controller added, "It's the power of 'what if' at your fingertips."

10

Doing More with Less—a Likely "What if"

Now that we are in a frame of mind to consider 'what-ifs,' it is worth spending some time examining a potential 'what-if' that is likely to inform the next few years of the business cycle. That scenario is one that involves doing more with less, as industries—especially the IT industry—look to the 'new way' instead of 'the new thing.'

"Less is more," gained fame as a dictum of the renowned architect Ludwig Mies van der Rohe. He was referring to building design, of course, but the maxim has proven its applicability to many fields. In recent times, "less is more" has become the operative paradigm in the IT realm. Overall, this will be a highly beneficial trend—because it will generate new kinds of collaboration and new kinds of creativity. But it will require a new mindset, along with new business intelligence solutions.

In recent years, IT departments rushed to acquire new technologies and platforms. Let's look, for example, at a prototypical high-functioning IT group: Over the past three years they would have implemented a leading enterprise resource planning (ERP) system, such as SAP, for automating standard processes like order management and financial transactions. This same organization may have implemented a customer relationship management system (CRM) to capture detailed customer and buying patterns. On the technical end, there is a corporate intranet and a data warehouse to collect data. By any measure, all of this represents a significant investment in "new new things."

Economic conditions have altered. The CFO of such an organization is typically looking back and trying to find a return in investment for these major technology expenditures. This, in turn, is causing the CIO to rethink recent purchases in terms of ROI.

The conclusion reached is inevitable: ROI can be generated by consolidation of past investments, i.e., by creating a whole that is substantially greater than the sum of its parts. It is actually quite simple to derive ROI by integrating customer, supply and financial data using data warehouses for storing the data and delivering it through a corporate intranet. This is what will bring ROI to the next level.

It may seem odd to some that the business benefits of integrating IT systems have not been realized yet. But this seeming "oversight" is understandable in terms of recent technological history. The lapse is actually an outgrowth of the proliferation of distributed systems, which really started in the late 1980's. Prior to distributed, or client/server systems, everything was centralized on a mainframe, and integration was almost unavoidable. The problem was that the lack of functionality and total cost of ownership (TCO) for these systems drove the need for more distributed systems. Everyone was focused on the functionality of the systems, so the integration—which was previously taken for granted—slipped away. The Internet has come a long way in providing an integrated platform and protocol, but software, in particular, is mainly still being sold as one-off solutions.

Now the prevailing question on everyone's mind is: How can we maximize the vast potential of the systems we've already got in place to create genuine business intelligence?

Data warehousing is a fairly mature discipline; the same can be said for online analytical processing (OLAP). At the same time, data mining has matured technically, but has minimal commercial acceptance. The future of business intelligence is a platform and set of tools that can integrate data warehousing, OLAP and data mining.

Another prevailing trend in business intelligence will be the move toward standardization. OLAP and data mining have been notorious for needing proprietary, non-standard databases. Database technologies have matured to the point where the argument of "my cube is better than your cube" is dead. Organizations are now able to take advantage of OLAP, data warehousing and data mining without risking proprietary obsolescence. As this is done, value is added.

Case Study

Producing parallel management accounts during a company reorganization of eighty subsidiaries in more than fifty countries is an overwhelming feat. However, with scenario planning supporting the creation of what is perceived to be the optimal new structure, the feat becomes far more manageable. A major banking institution monitoring the progress of its restructuring by using "what-if" scenarios.

Previously the organization would have been limited to working with Excel spreadsheets and multiple data models. By using a comprehensive business intelligence and performance management software suite, they were able to manage inter-related spreadsheets and perform calculations much faster. The time saved in creating reports enabled the reorganization team to focus on other important issues, such as analysis. It also enabled them to work collaboratively as a team, improving productivity.

The major advantage of the new breed of business intelligence tools that facilitate integration is that they enable organizations to get from *what* to *why* of their data. When an organization is managing the why's instead of the what's of their business, it is a simple matter to ascertain what is happening in your business. In the big picture it is also relatively trivial. Any reporting tool can tell you, "Sales are down twenty percent this quarter." The next question must be, "why?" Is there a product-related problem? Is there a glitch in a distribution channel? Is this a dip in one geographic area? Is this seasonal? Standard OLAP or reporting cannot tell you the reason. And in the past, getting to the reason required a group of statisticians using a very complex—one might almost say "mystical"—mining tool. With this functionality now available to the masses—and based on open standards—organizations can improve both the efficiency and effectiveness of the decision-making process. They can also drive down labor costs and expedite time to market.

Part of the beauty of the new generation of business tools is that they require minimal technological training. When these tools make use of open standards, many of the skills required by IT are already in place. From an end-user training perspective, the ease of use of OLAP has been translated to data mining. One caveat, however: organizations must be prepared to push decision-making further down in the organization, and they must provide the business training required to make this effective.

I have sometimes been asked whether I foresee a stumbling block to this dynamic in that some groups or individuals may be reluctant to share information, even within their own organization. This has been a risk since before computers. Information has always been a form of power-base. The new culture of collaboration must be driven from the top down. Yet, even with a clear edict from the CEO, there will be resistance. It is the job of senior management to properly align organizational structure and associated compensation plans to the new collaborative culture.

As for IT professionals, their job will be to choose and implement best-of-breed business intelligence solutions that make true collaboration feasible. When it comes to spending on new systems, decisions should be made with great care. Our current technology saturation has put the industry on a fairly stable plateau—in terms of Internet computing and large scale databases—for at least the next eighteen months. As one CFO recently said to me, "While there will always be pure technologists who want the 'new, new thing', the question should now be do they need it?"

Managers and all employees must realize that companies that collaborate with their data and their systems will be the leaders during this new age of integration.

You've Created It, Now Communicate It

Hans Christian Andersen started out by telling his stories in his small Danish town. Eventually, he was published and is recognized as one of the great children's authors ever. Imagine if Mr. Andersen had kept his stories in his head and never spoken them or written them down. What joys the world would have missed!

In business there are countless ideas, even moments of brilliance, that are never communicated. Maybe it is an accounts receivable manager who has an idea to shorten the collection cycle for forty percent of all customers. Maybe it is a product manager with the idea of bundling two products to increase the pull-through of a lagging product. Maybe it is a human resources manager with an idea for a new retention bonus program. All may be great ideas, but if they are not communicated they remain ideas instead of actions.

UNEMPOWERED EMPOWERMENT

Management trends of empowerment and quality management are supposed to push decision making further down in the organization. The idea is to bring the decision making closer to the actionable items, with the people who best understand what the impact will be.

Organizations will perform training on empowerment. They may design new compensation schemes to support empowerment. They may even create new organizations based on empowerment. But many organizations do not take into account two of the greatest obstacles to communication-enabled empowerment: time and information.

How do organizations attempt to empower employees?

1. Empowerment 'training'

2. Modifying compensation plans

3. Broadening decision scope

How many executives would argue with a proposition to shorten collection cycles or increase product revenue? Probably very few. Many of these propositions are never heard because of time constraints. Downsizing, cutbacks, consolidations and mergers have created a culture of bare-bones operations. There are barely enough hours to perform the operational tasks to keep the business going. This is like a basketball player being so fixated on dribbling that he keeps his head down staring at the ball to perfect his dribbling. Meanwhile, the opponent sneaks up and takes the ball from right under his nose. Organizations need to have the time to dribble with their heads up. They need time to take care of operational issues, but also need time to concentrate on longer-term issues. A major problem with first-time teenage drivers is to look only at the hood of their car at what is directly in front of them. Driving instructors will teach that you should be looking further out, hundreds of yards, and still have the peripheral vision to react to instant obstacles. To enable organizations to dribble with their heads up, they need more time. And time is something you cannot just buy.

A second obstacle to communication is information. This includes both the lack of information and low quality of information. There are probably many great conclusions that can be drawn by empowered managers, but they need the historical and real-time data to support their hypothesis. There is often a skeptical attitude about the quality of data as well. This leads to a risk-adverse environment. Many managers will not stick their necks out on a hunch. No one wants to be caught in a situation where they have to support a new idea without hard facts.

DATA GATHERING AND DATA DETAIL

The process of gathering data is very similar across departments and industries. There are certain nuances to each situation, but a four-step process is generally followed. First, one investigates the required sources of data. This can involve finding files and databases and determining what data is stored in what source. Also, part of this step is to assess the quality of the data. Does it have all the needed information or is some of it missing? Does it appear that all the fields have a consistent format or are formats assigned haphazardly (i.e. is the customer number always eight characters, or is it six in one system and eight in another)? Does some of the data just not make sense (are customer names in places where you expect vendors, etc.)?

Second, the data is collected to in one place. This gathering exercise takes in data from the various sources, such as the financial, supply and customer relationship systems, and creates a single place for the data. This consolidated system is often referred to as a data warehouse.

Data homogenizing is the third step. The data is correlated and indexed. The least common denominator of information, such as customer number or vendor name, is determined and used as the building block. Based this least common concept, the data can be compared across multiple business lines.

The fourth step is data optimization. With optimization, the data warehouse is configured to allow the fastest and most flexible reading of the data. Since the volumes are very large, care needs to be taken into building this design. In fact, a whole sub-industry of data warehouse architecture has been born to support this optimization process.

By following this four-step approach, the proper level of detail is available regardless of how the data needs to be shared. If a product manager needs detailed SKU-level data, it is available. If a human resource manager needs employee level information, it is available. If the COO needs top-line numbers only, they are also available.

By providing the proper level of data, managers can actually be empowered to make informed decisions. Next, though, it is necessary to share this information. An idea is only as good as the way in which it is communicated.

THE DRIVER, MECHANIC AND BUYER

Since the focus of using the gathered data is to measure and impact upon performance, organizations need to understand the best way to communicate this information. Not everyone in an organization needs a bound set of reports. Still others may not be satisfied with merely high-level reports.

When dealing with an automobile, three possible roles are: driver, mechanic, and buyer. This is a useful metaphor when looking at performance data.

The Driver

The main interface to an automobile for a driver is the dashboard. Dashboards for performance management are, as the name implies, very similar to the dashboard of an automobile. There are multiple high level indicators that can all be seen on one computer screen. The user of the dashboard does not need to navigate through multiple systems. Instead, it is all pre-assembled in the dashboard.

Similar to that of an automobile, the corporate dashboard represents a consolidation of inputs taken from multiple sources. The performance dashboard is suitable for upper management and executives, but will probably not provide the level of detailed required by line managers.

The Mechanic

Automobile mechanics deal in much higher levels of detail than drivers. They must be able to diagnose, reference and fix problems. This often requires detailed diagnostic tools, reference manuals, and a lot of know-how. Similarly, reports are the tool of choice for managers. Preferably, these reports are electronic and active. Active reports, compared to standard paper reports, allow drilling down (i.e., starting at product groups and moving down to SKUs) and pivoting (i.e., changing the columns and rows). Active reports also allow graphic representation such as pie and bar charts. All of the data in the dashboard view can be found in the reports, but the reports offer much more detail.

The Buyer

When buying a car, potential buyers will utilize a series of prepared documents such as window stickers, magazine write-ups and brochures to evaluate their purchasing options. Similarly, briefings are a tool that can be used by any stakeholders, internal (managers, executives, employees) and external (investors, regulators, business partners). Briefings, sometimes referred to as briefing books, are publication quality snapshots of the performance of an organization.

The Driver, Mechanic and Buyer

 Monitoring and real-time adjustments

 Diagnosing and fixing

 Evaluating and taking action

The briefing books are created from the same data as the reports and the dashboard. With the briefing books, a small set of relevant analysis chart and graphs, usually less than ten, are combined with an executive summary and commentary. Examples of relevant analysis for a briefing book are: time series—examining the performance of certain measures across a set time frame; ABC Ranking—grouping into high, medium and low performing groups based on products or customers; Outlier Analysis—defining and grouping together anomalies such as severe under or over performers; and Movement Analysis—combining a set time series and rankings to analyze group and individuals across time.

Like a good product brochure or magazine review of an automobile, a successful briefing book concisely represents the relevant facts so that an individual can understand the book with little or no guidance. Imagine having to need a class to read window stickers on a new car? The executive summary and commentary should present enough information to help with understanding, but not overburden the reader with theories.

The method of choice is to deliver a briefing book as a document, but it should also easily translate to a PowerPoint slide show for group review. Once again, this should use the same performance data.

One Stop Performance Management Shopping

Less than ten years ago, it was acceptable for an organization to purchase a financial system from one company, a supply chain system from another and maybe use a homegrown customer management system. In the 1990's, this changed with the broad acceptance of Enterprise Resource Planning (ERP) and Customer Relationship Management (CRM) systems. ERP vendors, such as SAP, PeopleSoft and JD Edwards, along with CRM vendors such as Siebel and Oracle, enabled organizations to rely on a single source for computerized applications. The concept is to reduce overhead and increase efficiency by providing standardized computer systems and achieving economies of scale by purchasing the systems from one vendor.

Performance management systems vendors are going through a similar process this decade. Traditionally, there have been islands of performance data created in an organization. The financial people may use one system for measuring performance, while another system is used by the supply side of the organization. Some of this was driven by the lack of flexibility in performance management systems. For example, many of the long-time financial applications, do not easily adapt to include non-financial data (customer, internal, and organizational data).

There is a growing trend for treating all performance data from one application. Much of this was driven out of the balanced scorecard concept, which some companies have adopted.

Performance management systems that will support today's financial and non-financial needs absolutely require the ability to do this using a single tool. This will avoid the islands of information that many organizations are caught in now. This 'one stop shopping' concept will enable greater performance.

Prior to the supermarket, families would have to go to a butcher shop, baker shop, general store and such to do what can now be accomplished in a single visit to supermarket. One could argue that performance management systems are just now breaking ground on their first supermarkets. During this transition time, organization will lean on the performance management systems already in place (if any), but they will eventually move to the 'one stop shopping' concept.

CLOSING THE LOOP

Having the proper performance data organization and allowing open communication through dashboards, reports and briefings will enable organizations to achieve higher levels of performance management and directly impact the bottom line.

The next logical step is to allow this performance management information to freely flow into actionable items or a business plan/budget. If an organization discovers that a particular product line is lagging and wishes to discontinue it, they should be able to model this directly and create a budget and forecast.

Case Study

The vast activities of one of the world's top chemical-pharmaceutical companies' range from healthcare and agriculture to polymers and chemicals. Due to the company's global presence, enterprise budgeting and controlling present a significant challenge. Enterprise reporting, for example, must account for heterogeneous system environments, multiple languages, currencies, and even time zones. A customized information system based on planning and analysis software was developed to automate every step in the reporting process.

Flexible analysis was a key element for selecting this information system. It imports relevant business data into its associated companies and transfers this data back to headquarters–and whether calculating key figures or creating analyses and evaluations, data can be transferred and analyzed. The system delivers flowing, problem-free global reporting workflows despite time differences and the headquarters now has immediate access to relevant figures.

Example of an Executive Dashboard

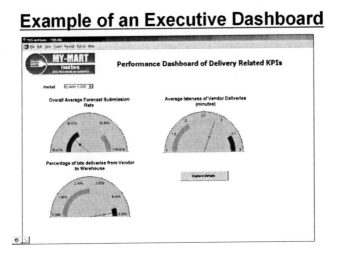

Closing the loop between understanding performance and taking actionable items will allow even greater efficiency and reduce workflow redundancy.

Lack of time and information often prevents managers and executives from coming up with new ideas for improving performance. When performance measurements and areas for improvement are discovered, there is still the challenge of communicating this information to the whole organization. Organizations need to select the proper delivery mechanism for performance data. Executives will require a summarized dashboard. Managers will require active reports. Stakeholders, internal and external, will benefit from briefings. By properly deploying this information, organizations can put the tools in place to empower management.

Conclusion

The Chief Performance Officer is a role whose time has come. The disciplines of managing corporate performance are becoming more relevant to organizations of all sizes.

Many organizations may already have a group or department measuring parts of their performance. In particular, the finance organization monitors and measures financial performance. Some leading organizations have gone well beyond the financial metrics to include other key performance indicators. Far more organizations, though, are not leveraging the corporate assets of metrics, which are locked up in computer systems, files, and human brains.

In the early days of data processing, computer programmers were seen as a specialized group of people performing specific technical tasks. Programs were created for one off reasons and soon the organization had a large amount of data and information, which was untapped for contributing to the bottom line. In the 1980's the role of the chief information officer became popular to provide a strategic use of information for the organization. Issues such as architecture, outsourcing, standards, and reusability became keys to managing the information of an organization. The 1980's were also the time when data processing became information technology.

Currently, much of what can be though of as the tools of the CPO are referred to generally as business intelligence. Business intelligence is a term that grew out of technologies to support decisions and includes such topics as data warehousing, online analytical processing, reporting and data mining. Most of these topics are being handled by an information technology organizations, which in many cases limits the business applicability.

As outlined throughout this book, the CPO is only part technologist. The CPO must use all the business, technological, and communications tools at his or her command to provide comprehensive and comprehendible interpretation of performance at all levels, but particularly at the C-level of an organization.

Will organizations adopt the formal term CPO? As they did with the chief knowledge officer, many will; others will still have the role of CPO, but that person will be called by another name. In any case, organizations must realize that as pressures such as competition, regulation, velocity of change, and globalization grow, this will only further emphasize the necessity of the CPO.

0-595-28057-9